DATE DUE

JE 7 06			

Couplets From
Kabīr

COUPLETS FROM KABĪR
(*Kabīr Dohe*)

being originals in Devanāgarī script and translations
into rhymed English verse of three hundred selected
Dohe and brief commentary in prose under each.

The couplets are the eyes of wisdom
Take heed I aver so
Without their aid, the knotty problems
Of the world will not go.

KABĪR

Couplets From
Kabīr

Edited, Translated and Compiled by
G.N. DAS

With a Foreword by
RANGANATH MISHRA
Former Chief Justice, Supreme Court of India

With an Introduction by
J.M. MOHANTY

MOTILAL BANARSIDASS PUBLISHERS
PRIVATE LIMITED ● DELHI

First Edition: 1991
Reprint: Delhi, 1997, 1998, 1999, 2001

35-1 (Cloth)
25-4 (Paper)

ble at:
MOTILAL BANARSIDASS
236, 9th Main III Block, Jayanagar, Bangalore 560 011
41 U.A. Bungalow Road, Jawahar Nagar, Delhi 110 007
8 Mahalaxmi Chamber, Warden Road, Mumbai 400 026
120 Royapettah High Road, Mylapore, Chennai 600 004
Sanas Plaza, 1302 Baji Rao Road, Pune 411 002
8 Camac Street, Kolkata 700 017
Ashok Rajpath, Patna 800 004
Chowk, Varanasi 221 001

Printed in India
BY JAINENDRA PRAKASH JAIN AT SHRI JAINENDRA PRESS,
A-45 NARAINA, PHASE-I, NEW DELHI 110 028
AND PUBLISHED BY NARENDRA PRAKASH JAIN FOR
MOTILAL BANARSIDASS PUBLISHERS PRIVATE LIMITED,
BUNGALOW ROAD, DELHI 110 007

DEDICATION

The
illustrious
saint-poet, Kabīr,
from whose lips flowed
effortlessly and extempore
thousands of songs and coup-
lets replete with spiritual message and
worldly wisdom, and who professed one-
ness of the entire humanity and the religion of humanism and
craved well-being of all his fellow men on earth wept as follows:

All the people are living happily
Eating and sleeping soundly
Dāsa Kabīr alone is sorrowing
Awake and weeping profusely.

KABĪR DOHĀ

Kabīr was weeping not for himself but for his
fellowmen, countrymen, and entire humanity's
well-being and salvation. In honour of the
sixth centenary of this celebrated saint-poet
which was observed last year throughout
the country this humble work of
rhymed verse translation in English
of three hundred selected couplets from the entire cross-sec-
tion of his work is dedi-
cated to the PEOPLE OF
INDIA where he was
born six hundred
ears ago from
today.

FOREWORD

I have been asked to write a foreword to the series of Kabīr's *Dohe* rendered into English by Mr. Gananath Das.

Kabīr had no schooling—formal or informal but he was a born saint-poet. He transcended the bounds of religion, rose to greatest heights in his spiritual thoughts and broke into spontaneous lyrics and *bhajans*. Kabir's apparently simple *dohe* contain the essence of the great of philosophical ideas. The level of divinity in him is clearly reflected in his *dohe* and *bhajans*. Both of these abound in narration of elevating experiences of his life and illustrate his anxiety for generation of devotion for God in the common man. Kabīr's mortal body, as the popular belief goes, was claimed both by the Hindus and the Muslims for performance of the last rites but the same vanished and a beautiful flower full bloom was found at the site.

The translator often fails to convey the true meaning of the original writing. It is particularly so when the theme is based upon divine experience or deep religious sentiments. Mr. Das has done a neat rendering of the *dohe*. This has perhaps been possible as he has got a clear insight into the corridors of divinity and is possessed of sufficient command over the English language.

Kabīr's *dohe* have a direct appeal to the heart. Familiar and common place illustrations and references bring about an immediate impact on the reader. In today's world of fallen standards of life sans religion, Kabīr's *dohe* in English medium would reach a larger spectrum of readers and help in generation of an adequate metabolic force.

I hope the series will receive universal appreciation and provide encouragement to Mr. Das to devote his full attention in retired life to this neglected wing of life today.

Supreme Court of India　　　　　　　　　RANGANATH MISRA
New Delhi
November 20, 1990

CONTENTS

FOREWORD vii

INTRODUCTION xi

PREFACE xvii

ACKNOWLEDGEMENTS xxxi

APPRECIATION xxxiii

TEXT

On Gurudeva or the Preceptor 1

On *Iṣṭadeva* or the Supreme Lord 5

On *Prema Bhakti* or Love-devotion to the Lord 11

On *Ātma Samarpaṇa* or Self Surrender to the Lord 24

On *Ācaraṇa* or Maintenance of Conduct
and Character 29

On Mind and Its Control 42

On *Māyā* or Illusion 48

On *Cetabāni* or Warning 49

On *Vyaṅga* or Sarcastic Utterances 68

On *Mṛtyu* or Death 76

On *Biraha* or Yearning for the Lord 81

On *Kāma* or Lust, Sex, Women   85

On *Satsaṅga* or Association with the Noble
and Righteous   86

On *Paropkāra* or Assistance and Charity to Others   88

On *Upadeśa* or Advice   91

On *Darśana* or Philosophical and Spritual Topics   101

On *Jīvātmā, Paramātmā* and *Mokṣa* or Soul,
Supreme Soul and Salvation   113

On *Garva* or Pride   117

On *Boli* or Words of Mouth   120

On *Moha* or Bonds of Earth (Attachment)   122

Miscellaneous   123

Glossary   127

Bibliography   133

INTRODUCTION

Kabīr, the famous 15th Century Bhakti-poet from Uttar Pradesh, is said to have composed a large number of *bhajanas* and *dohās*, which subsequently became famous all over India. Many of these have been translated into different Indian languages, including English. Particularly the *bhajanas* are available in many translated versions. But not so *dohās*. Therefore, Shri Das's attempts to translate the *dohās* into English for the benefit of a wider public is a very welcome act. Shri Das, it may be pointed out, is eminently fit for the job both by taste and scholarship. He has translated Kabīr's *bhajanas* and *dohās* into Oriya, and also written a fine, scholarly book on Kabīr in the same language. It is only a pleasure to record that Shri Das has broadened his activities with love and ability.

The *dohās* are pithy poetic statements and they illustrate the poet's personality and attitudes as nothing else can. *Kabīr's dohās* have particularly a multi-faceted structure. They have wit and intelligence, and a tendency to project multiple meanings through apt use of imagery. But what is most remarkable is, the *dohās* are full of worldly wisdom which steadily elevates into a philosophic understanding of life. The *dohās* please and provoke and always aim at a benign understanding of life and life's problems.

In fact the poet's primary concern is with the individual who should know how correctly and hence how peacefully he may live in the society. What man needs to cultivate to live in harmony with his fellow-beings in the society, are such common-sense virtues which are always around us and which are often forgotten in action. These are forgiveness, humility, gentleness, patience as well as love and compassion for others and a habit to listen to prudent and wise advice. Misdeeds are our enemies, the poet proclaims again and again. One is prone to fall into quagmire of selfishness, lustfulness and laziness, and man's propensity to move into dark areas of conduct is more than his desire to move out of it. Liberality of mind and heart as well as liberality in outlook are often talked of, but little practised, though, the poet points out, they provide important social parameters of living. The pull on man is from adverse directions—upward and downward, and as is natural, the downward-pull is stronger than the upward-pull. It not only requires strength but also will, strong concentrated will, to move upward to freedom of light and air. The poet presents it graphically in the symbolic account of saint, chaste woman and warrior, walking on 'hard unbeaten track' always in the danger of missing their track and getting completely undone.

> The saint, chaste woman and warrior—
> They are comparable to none,
> They tread on hard, unbeaten track
> And when they fall, lo! completely undone. [76]

In fact the poet is keenly aware of the relevance of good name and fame while living in the society, and life should be so motivated as to have both in good time.

> When born on earth you cried aloud
> Others laughed in glee
> Do not in life do any such deed
> That they will laugh at thee. [140]

To acquire knowledge is essential, the poet points out, but not an end. To study, to know, to participate effectively in discourses are no doubt useful activities. But they become more useful when they are used to equip the mind with power to control and regulate action as well as speech.

> Thus says Kabīr,
> The king, the beggar, and the saint
> All are disconsolate
> Only he who controls his mind
> Is happy and content. [104]

And elsewhere he speaks of speech which is like a priceless gem,

> Speech is the most precious wealth
> If you know what to speak,
> Diamond you can buy with money
> Speech is priceless gem to seek. [229]

Thus correct living is synonymous with good action, good speech as well as good habits. One cannot live even in routine matters, as he likes, and then claim that he is living correctly. Day to day routine matters are as much important as an understanding of or approach to life, because while considering the totality of living, the poet maintains, the smaller, less serious occupations are as much relevant as higher, more serious objectives. Thus he points out what to eat and how much to eat. Meat-eating is bad, he says, irrespective of whether it is fowl, beef or venison, because it never leads to 'salvation', and he prays to god to give him just that amount of food as he needs for his family, guests and himself, and no more. In fact he is angry about killing animals. It should not be done, he declares, and asks the priest sarcastically why can't he himself chop off his own head instead of the animal's, so that he himself can go to heaven in the place of the latter. There are other references too, such as his dislike for begging money or asking for favour. His statement is pithy and pointed in this respect.

> Words of love and welcome dry up
>> In moments and for ever
> As soon as you stretch your hand
>> And beg for the smallest favour. [156]

These are habits, but they refine the mind and promote cheerfulness and happiness. But cheerful man is rare, and happy man is most rare, the poet points out, because both cheerfulness and happiness are projections of mind which depend upon how best the mind has been controlled and motivated and to what extent it has been able to contemplate with equanimity on matters of life and death. In the *dohās* the awareness of death is strong, and it surfaces again and again. All of us are in the clutches of death, the poet says, and anybody can be nipped off in the bud. It is a matter of time when one goes, but go one must.

> At the falling dry old leaf
>> The tender leaf does sneer,
>> Says the falling leaf—
> 'Today my turn, tomorrow yours
>> Have patience, O my dear.' [187]

But death is not the end; the poet does not accept it as the last word. There is a possibility that one may die, that is, annihilate himself, but only to take a newer and richer shape. In a *dohā*, strongly reminiscent of Donne, the British metaphysical poet, the poet points out this paradox,

> Do so meditate on the Lord
> The flow of it will not drain
> Do die that death, O my friend
> You shall not die again. [168]

This is a matter of devotion—to what extent one can motivate his mind towards that end. But once achieved, this will provide the strongest counter against death. Devotion is synonymous with love—love of the Lord, and in its finality it is annihilation—annihilation of self. The poet expresses his devotion to the 'Lord' in unmistakable terms,

> Before the Lord I shall offer
> Candles of knowledge, bells of prayer,
> Where shines the Lord in eternal glow
> His slave Kabīr stands there. [261]

In fact real devotion is to be achieved, the poet says. It is like putting one's foot into fire, because one cannot know how fire burns unless the foot is put into it. Or it is like the deer's attraction towards the hunter—the deer listens to the hunter's song only to lose its life to the hunter's gun.

These are all intertwined. Man moves through death to a condition beyond death, and that condition of mind that dwells on devotion is as intimate and intense as one's love towards his beloved. In fact the knowledge of love is best knowledge, the poet says, and whoever possesses it is the real wise man. This is unlike the knowledge about scriptures—it is deeper and more complex and ultimately leads to self-knowledge and control of mind. The poet's expression in this respect is eloquent,

> Mind-bird flies here and there
> Tasting mundane pleasure
> As long as the knowledge-falcon
> Has not taken it over. [111]

Elsewhere the poet compares the 'proud mind' with elephant and points out that as one can 'hook the elephant' the mind can be controlled likewise. It is both a condition of mind as well as an understanding of life. Love and devotion blossom into knowledge, and knowledge illumines the recesses of mind, which ultimately provides that serene and benign happiness which alone is conducive to the growth of that spirit which helps man to see into the 'life of things'. This is the condition of mind of a seer. Kabīr's poetry grows from social realities where he knows how or to what extent grief, pain and disaster undo one's life and how consequences of a man's action always go with him. But finally it comes to a level of contemplation where immediate and apparently important things cease to matter, and where the life's understanding flowers into a vision of great illumination and power.

To say that Kabīr 'synthesized the religious spirit underlying Islam and Hinduism', is a limited commentary on Kabīr's poetry. Even to say that Kabīr's poems expressed 'folk-wisdom as well as mystic whisperings of love' ('An Anthology of Indian Literature', Ed. J.B. Alphonso-Karkala, ICOR, 1987) is not enough. Kabīr has given what every great poet in the world has given—a contemplation on the structure of life as well as an insight into the essence of living.

JATINDRA MOHAN MOHANTY

PREFACE

Sant Kabīr has been acclaimed as the most outstanding of the saint-poets of *Bhakti* cult (devotion) and mysticism of 15th Century India. He was born at Vārāṇasī (Banaras) in the year 1389 just six hundred years ago from now.

According to a legend a new born fair child was noticed afloat a giant lotus leaf in the Lahara Tāla lake on the outskirts of Vārāṇasī by a Muslim couple, Nīrū and Nimmā by name. They were childless and being attracted by the fair, playful child they considered the foundling as God's gift, and picked it up and reared it as their foster-child.

This child grew up to be the celebrated saint Kabīr and was acclaimed as such throughout the world for the large number of his utterings of *Dohās* (couplets) and *bhajanas* (devotional songs) of great spiritual fervour and poetic quality.

Young Kabīr spurned the idea of having formal education. He was convinced that all that one needed to learn was the letters that composed 'Rāma', the name of the deity he adored and worshipped. There was no need to learn the entire alphabet, much less the books written in it. He declared he would not touch paper and ink. Thus he remained illiterate.

He gained his deep insight and wisdom from the book of life and extensive contact with saints and seers of various faiths over a number of years. Vārāṇasī being an important seat of spiritual practices attracted leaders of various faiths. Thus Hindus flocked in great numbers there and the members of its various sects—viz. *Vaiṣṇavas, Śaivas, Śāktas, Gāṇapatyas, Yogīs, Nātha-panthīs, Tāntrikas,* etc. So did the followers of Sūfism, Buddhism, Jainism and other religions. Saints and seers in large number visited Vārāṇasī continuously. Some of them made Vārāṇasī their head-quarters, establishing their monasteries, mosques, or temples dedicated to their respective Gods. Kabīr had the benefit of long association and communion with them, association that enriched his innate spiritual faculties.

Kabīr, according to a legend, was born of a Brahmin widow who abandoned her new born child on the Lahara Tāla lake. Growing up in the foster parents' home he imbibed knowledge of Islamic faith and ethnics. In his youth he was attracted by the

liberal outlook of the famous spiritual leader, Rāmānanda, who
had set up a monastery on the Ganges and drew persons from
different sects for spiritual guidance. Kabīr was fortunate to
have him as his preceptor and was able to enrich his spiritual
faculty by his able and generous guidance.

Although Kabīr accepted Gosvāmi Rāmānanda as his preceptor, he did not join the community of the preceptor's cult,
or for that matter, any cult whatsoever. Kabīr's devotion for
the Lord is qualified, nay, dominated by love. Thus he says:

> Devotion without love for the Lord
> If held as devotion
> You do so out of insolence
> Wasting your life anon. [Elsewhere]

And, as a devout lover of the Lord he wondered—

> Deep and strong is not my love
> Nor have I a beauteous face
> I do not know my Beloved's ways
> And if I can get His grace. [47]

It is said that Kabīr was influenced in this respect by the belief
of the Vaiṣṇava cult of the Hindu faith and also the Sūfī cult of
the Islamic faith in both of which devotion to the Lord is suffus-
ed with love for Him. To that extent Kabīr is seen to have
deviated from the pure *Bhakti* cult of his preceptor, Rāmānanda.

Kabīr was born at a crucial juncture in Indian history when
Muslim rule was gaining ground in the country, simultaneously
with the spread of Islam. Hinduism was on the wane. There were
frequent clashes and feuds between the two communities on
account of misunderstandings arising out of petty quarrels and
also due to differences in religious practices of the two faiths and
rigid orthodox views on both sides.

Kabīr by his innate talent was able to bring about a synthesis
of both the great faiths, taking the best from each. He also took
note of the weak points of both the faiths and through his *dohās*
and songs tried to help restore understanding and tolerance
between the two communities instead of engaging in futile feuds
over inessential matters of detail relating to their respective
faiths and differences of caste, creed, community, colour, clime,
languages, etc.—matters which Kabīr considered as irrelevant.

He succeeded, to a great extent, in this effort at allaying the misunderstanding between the two communities by focusing their attention on the fundamental principles enunciated by both the faiths, viz. love and devotion to the Lord, love of fellowmen, compassion for all beings, and the moral principles of good and noble living which are identical in both cases.

Soon Kabīr started attracting a crowd of admirers and followers by his songs and couplets which he composed and recited extempore to the accompaniment of his musical instrument, Tāmburā. These verses were imbued with deep spiritual fervour. Many of them were full of wisdom and showed them how to lead a pure and happy life. Kabīr composed his verses in the common language of the people. His similes and metaphors were homely and natural. There was nothing artificial or learned about them. The result was that his verses made an instant appeal to the common people of his time. Kabīr had not only a fine sense of music but was endowed with a melodious voice which lent charm to his songs and couplets.

Kabīr's admirers and followers would learn his couplets by heart and sang them with feeling and devotion alone and in company. That is how the songs and couplets saw the light of day and have come down to us. This is also why we notice some variations in the language of the *dohās* and songs collected from different sources.

Kabīr has been credited with the authorship of several thousands of *bhajanas* (songs) and *dohās* (couplets) which effortlessly flowed from his lips. Some three hundred of the songs have found place in the holy Granth Saheb of the Sikh faith. His diction and style are distinctly his own. Most of the original couplets have been taken from the works of Dr. Ram Kumar Verma, Dr. Sham Sunder Das and Ācārya Hazari Prasad Dvwedy. Professor Ram Kumar Verma has this to say about the genius of Kabīr in his well-known work "Kabīr, Biography and Philosophy":

"Kabīr has been acknowledged as one of the greatest poets who has given the minutest details of the whole history of human thought which is amazing and amusing to contemplate upon. The poet does not *write* but *utters* and his speech scores much above the authority of all scholarship of written thought. In short Kabīr was 'not of an age, but for all times'."

Scholars all over the world have marvelled at the depth and
sweep of his insight and his deep concern for the well-being of
humanity. It would be extremely difficult to summarise in a few
words this rich complexity of his thought and vision. His range
is wide and his insight astounding. The wonder becomes all the
great when one remembers that he was an illiterate person.

There is practically no aspect of human life which Kabīr has
left untouched in his couplets.

One may wonder what prompted Kabīr to do what he did.
Why was Kabīr so anxious to do that? It is quite evident that
Kabīr was anxious not only for his own salvation but that of his
fellowmen for whom he had deep love and sympathy. In the
following dohā Kabīr declares categorically—

> Standing in the open market,
>   Says Kabīr, I crave good of all
> With none am I intimate
>   And to none inimical. [Elsewhere]

and also

> Says Kabīr,
> I bring the message of salvation
>   To the Hindu and Mussalman
> And of snapping the bonds of the earth
>   But I am with no one. [251]

In the above *dohā* [251] Kabīr specifically mentions Hindus
and Muslims because they were the two principal communities
of the time, but the truth is he had the whole human society in
view when he wrote verses like these.

A few salient points from the broad spectrum of the message
conveyed in the couplets may be highlighted here:

In his couplets and songs Kabīr firmly proclaimed the oneness
of humanity. All men, he says, are creatures of the same
Almighty Father, hail from the same land (heaven) and are made
of the same five elements.

Differences and barriers that men have created for themselves
are false. The following couplets go to establish this:

> Same is the semen, skin, urine
>> Same is the blood and bone
> From single source we all are born
>> How one is a Śūdra, the other a Brahman? [Elsewhere]

and says Kabīr,

> All are born as human beings
>> That is what we all know
> The cunning deceptor has made some 'Sūda'
>> Devising castes high and low. [65]

and also—

> We all hail from the same land
>> And reach here on earth
> Touched by the winds that blow here
>> Each pursues his own path. [168]

One of his significant messages is that man has been created in the image of God, the soul in him (*Jīvātmā*) being a part of the Supreme Soul (*Paramātmā*). Man must, therefore, cleanse his mind and heart as that is the abode of God in him. He should not expect God to reside in an unclean house. He should also shed all doubts of his mind.

The following couplets make this abundantly clear:

> Like fragrance in the heart of flower
>> In you the Lord dwells
> Musk is in the navel of the deer
>> Like deer you seek Him in the grass. [14]

> The Lord dwells in the heart of men
>> Like the pupil in the eye
> Fools this wisdom never gain
>> They seek him far and nigh. [16]

> If you want to see the face
>> You must keep the mirror clean
> But if the mirror is kept unclean
>> You cannot see the face therein. [Elsewhere]

> You have the mirror in your heart
>> But the face you cannot find
> You can see the visage there
>> If you dispel the doubts of mind. [Elsewhere]

According to Kabīr, the ultimate aim of man is to realise the Supreme Soul (God) or, in other words, attain salvation and he can succeed if he cleanses his mind, abandons anger, pride, lust, attachment and ego, loves his fellowmen and makes earnest effort to realise Him. These ideas are clearly reflected in the following couplets:

> Says Kabīr, you work and produce
>> Feed yourself and others too
> No religion is of greater value
>> Than love of beings around you. [Elsewhere]
> If your pride you cannot forsake
>> What use discarding attachment
> Pride doth the sage unmake
>> It eats up all, sinner and saint. [Elsewhere]

Kabīr believed with every conviction that God cannot be realised without first cleaning up of the mind and heart of the aspirant. He declared elsewhere in categorical terms:

> "*Hari nā mile bin hirde suddha*"
> You cannot get the Lord
> If your heart is impure.

He was anxious his fellowmen realise this truth. That is the reason why he has tried to deal with almost all the facets of human life and conduct as reflected in the everyday life of man. For, as it has been aptly said:

> "The great moments of heroism and sacrifice are rare. It is the little habits of common-place intercourse that make the great sum of life and sweeten or make bitter the journey."

And—

[Gardiner]

> "...the next is very much what we make it; we seem to be building our future in terms of our character here."

[Thomas Lodge]

And also—

> "...a life in which conduct does not fairly well accord with principles is a silly life."

[Arnold Benette]

In his songs (*bhajanas*) and *dohās* (couplets) Kabīr has, therefore, dealt with almost all conceivable aspects of human life. In his inimitable diction and style he has warned and exhorted his fellowmen to make every effort to avoid the pitfalls of life.

Kabīr laid great emphasis on purity of the mind. Man then becomes as simple as a child. And then God Himself runs after him and fulfils all his desires, including salvation. He considered purity even more rewarding than devotion.

> Says Kabīr, I have cleansed my mind
>> Pure as Ganges water
> The Lord now runs after me, I find,
>> Calling 'Kabīr, Kabīr!' [108]

> He who controls and cleans his mind
>> And makes it meditate on the Lord
> He again becomes as simple as child
>> Does wealth of purity hoard. [Elsewhere]

In many of his *dohās* Kabīr has emphasised that man is to reap as he will sow in life:

> You shall reap as you will sow
>> Is Lord Rāma's rule of law
> Sure salvation he will gain
>> Who acts as he does avow. [87]

According to Kabīr, one must be clean not only in his deeds, but also in his thought and words. In this he is one with what is laid down in the *Sanātana* Hindu religion as ideal conduct—in thought, word and deed. He has laid great stress on controlling the mind and also the tongue:

> Harsh word is worst of all
>> Burns its target to ash
> Sweet word is like heaven's Nectar
>> It pleases, cools, does not harass. [289]

And also:

> I have weighed and watched with care
>> Sweetness of all kind

That of the tongue is sweeter far
    If you use it well, you mind. [290]

On the importance of maintaining good conduct and character, Kabīr says:

Character is man's only asset
    His flesh no use to any one
His bone not fit for ornament
    And skin not fit for the drum. [89]

And also:

Whoever steadies his body and mind
    And tongue and conduct too
Shall earn fathomless wealth of wisdom
    None can gauge its value. [74]

Kabīr has again and again pointed out that even if the aspirant is able to control his mind, word and deed but fails to abandon pride, he will never succeed in his spiritual aspiration:

To kill your pride you take all pains
    Pride causes fall of man
       **   **   **
                       [Elsewhere]

He who has banished anger
    And also pride from mind
To every one is kind and dear
    Has no enemy to find. [285]

Similarly, Kabīr has warned his fellowmen against falling a prey to lust:

Lust it is, that assails all
    None can ward its pull
Scarce the man who does escape
    If by God's grace he is cool. [205]

Kabīr declared and warned in unmistakable terms that human life is not granted again and again. It is a rare prize won by good conduct and clean living in other inferior lives. If the boon of human life once received is not properly utilised, it slips out of hand. Man has the chance to pave the way for the soul in him (*Jīvātma*) to unite with the Supreme Soul (*Parmātamā*) by his own efforts in this life, or to slide back into inferior lives in the birth-death cycle if he pursues the wrong way. He must beware of this and follow the right path for his own salvation, in his thoughts, words and deeds (manasā, karmaṇā, vācā). There is no time for him to lose in indolence or in evil deeds. For, no one knows when he would be smoothered by death.

> Human life is so very precious
>   We do not get it again
> Like ripe fruit that drops from tree,
>   Can it ever rejoin? [255]

This conviction was so deep-seated in Kabīr and his concern for the welfare of all humanity so great that in the following *dohā* he expresses his deep sorrow to find man falling prey to the wiles of the world and to the evils within him, evils like lust, anger, greed attachment and pride (the five powerful enemies of man):

> Says Kabīr, I weep on seeing
>   The grind stone at work
> For not a grain comes out whole
>   From the grinding trap. [Elsewhere]

The simile expresses in graphic terms the lot of man who is reduced to nothingness by the evil forces operating in the world and in himself. Kabīr likens the two slabs of the grind stone to the two evil forces that break men to pieces.

It will be noticed that the *dohās* included here deal not merely with matters relating to the spirit but also to those relating to day to day life of man, to those of common sense and of apparently common place importance, and the like. Kabīr held that careful and clean living among neighbours and members of society as well as observance of simple rules of good conduct such as non-covetousness, self-restraint, honesty and straightforwardness and practising mercifulness, love and compassion, love to fellowmen would lead one to contentment in life. And, according to Kabīr, contentment is the most precious wealth of man:

> Cattle, wealth and gold and silver
>> All such wealth you mind
> Are like dust before contentment
>> That is the best wealth you will find. [237]

And, contentment and peace of mind will, Kabīr implies, help man to have that poise of mind which is so much necessary for the success and progress of spiritual attainment. And that is why Kabīr has laid stress on these matters of apparently common place importance. It may be worthwhile to repeat:

> "The great moments of heroism and sacrifice are rare. It is the little habits of common place intercourse that make the great sum of life and sweeten or make bitter the journey."   [Gardiner]

Self-controlled man can contemplate and meditate on the Lord and not a man beset with worries and immersed in worldly affairs. We can easily guess, therefore, why Kabīr has laid such great emphasis on cleaning the mind and heart and has embraced in his utterances all the numerous aspects of everyday life of man which hinder the control of mind and heart. Thus these apparently common-place matters are not really common-place. For, the ultimate aim of attaining salvation, the state of equanimity of the mind, assumes great importance.

The following couplets clearly establish the love and sympathy that Kabīr cherished in his heart for every man lost in the ways of the world and the depth of his grief at the sorrows suffered by him. That is why he poured out his heart in innumerable songs and couplets which can be easily understood and grasped by the common man for his benefit—

> I am devoted to the one alone
>> I am with every one
> All are mine and I am with all
>> Allen to me there is none. [Elsewhere]

Animal nature is to live
  For selfish ends alone
To die for others, if need be,
  As human nature is known. [95]

And that is also why Kabīr was so concerned with the welfare of the common man and, ultimately, with his salvation. In the following couplet, one of his most significant, he says:

Says Kabīr,
  I cried at my birth, others laughed in glee
    Do such deeds that when you depart from earth
  The others will cry for losing you
    While you will laugh in mirth. [Elsewhere]

In the couplets included in the present work strains of all these ideas and others of this multifaceted genius can be seen and in a style and a diction peculiarly his own.

The world today is in the grip of disputes and strifes, clashes and bloodshed on a vast scale owing to conflicts—linguistics, religious, racial, political and economic. The sense of values is at its lowest ebb. Even petty personal quarrels are leading people to violence and brutalities, the like of which were never seen before.

The message of *Sant* Kabīr will be of immense help as it was in the past to face this grim situation. It will help fostering understanding, love and fellow-feeling among the warring peoples and the erring individuals. They need, therefore, be propagated among the peoples of the world as widely, urgently and effectively as possible.

And that is why one feels like invoking *Sant* Kabīr to be re-born in India today as William Wordsworth (1770-1850) invoked John Milton (1608-74) urging him to return and restore the lost glory of the English people:

  "Milton thou shouldst be living at this hour
    England hath need of thee:
  **   **   **

We are selfish men
  O raise us up, return to us again.

And give us manners, virtue, freedom, power."
** ** **

This is applicable *mutatis mutandis* to Kabīr too. We need to
replace only the two initial words of the opening two lines of
Wordsworth's poem:

Kabīr thou shouldst be living at this hour
India and the World hath need of thee:
etc.   etc.   etc.

For, like the Englishman of Wordsworth's day, we too, in our
country, have fallen greatly in every walk of life in our conduct,
in our character, in our thought, in our moral sense.

And the current wave of corruption, the fall in standard of
moral sense, and clashes, violence and feuds among individuals
and communities and countries stemming from the divisive
forces discussed earlier are not confined to any particular region
or country. This is widespread over all the countries of the
world.

Kabīr not only had the power of his tongue with which he
uttered his message that inspired his fellowmen to follow the
path of righteousness fearlessly but he had also the guts to stand
up to the wrath of the powerful Brahmin priests and also the
omnipotent Sultan of Delhi. He did not deviate from his convic-
tions and path of righteousness despite threats and real danger
to his life. Like a true saint he was fearless to the core. From the
following couplets one can easily imagine his mettle:

Some kill the cock, others the goat
They say it is all proper
To the Lord all creatures are dear
To escape, what excuse will they offer? [153]

And

The donkey is far better than Brahmin
Dog is better than other castes
The cock is better than the Mullah
They wake the people by their blasts. [180]

Kabīr did not care for persecution by the Brahmin priests and the Sultan whose wrath he faced without flinching. Considering the times of Kabīr, one can easily imagine how brave he was as a true *Sant*. To utter such a 'blasphemy' in the presence of the Brahmin priests and the Mullahs, both of whom caused him to be hauled up before the Sultan, Kabīr must be admired to have been 'born with bones in his tongue'.

We need men of such extraordinary calibre to inspire our people at this critical hour of falling standards of moral values in every walk of life.

Hence the need for invoking Kabīr to return to us at this critical hour.

If we lend our ear to one of the finest examples of universal brotherhood of man advocated by Kabīr in the following oft quoted poem, we shall unhesitatingly bid for the widest possible circulation of Kabīr's couplets replete with the same spirit in order to cope with the current wave of communal discord not only in our country but in many parts of the world—

> If Khudā lives only in Masjid.
> who looks after the rest of the world?
> If Rāma is lodged in the temple idol
> who takes care of the universe?
> Is East the abode of Harī,
> and West that of Allāh?
> Search your heart for both of them
> there live both Karīm and Rām.
> They are one and the same
> Creator of the Universe.
> Men and women are His image
> and Kabīr is son of both Rām and Karīm,
> his preceptors are Guru and Pīr alike.

> [Translated by G.N. Das]

How relevant is Kabīr to the present day world torn by prejudice, intolerance and bigotry!

And I feel confident, that through Sant Kabīr's message of peace and tranquility, we would succeed to drive away the divisive forces and bring back the spirit of love and fellow-feeling not only among the peoples of India but the peoples of the entire world. His words, his style, his numbers have the power to change us, transform us.

Such a true saint, such a heart touching poet as Kabīr deserves all the attention for the benefit of mankind.

With this hope in mind I have in a humble way undertaken the work. I shall deem my labours amply rewarded if the books in the series reach the people on as wide a scale as possible, and help them understand *Sant* Kabīr's message.

Under each of the translated *dohās* (couplets) has been given a few lines in prose indicating the background/implication of the message the saint-poet wished to convey in order to help the reader to grasp the same.

G.N. DAS

ACKNOWLEDGEMENTS

I am deeply indebted to Shri B.N. Pande, the erudite Ex-Governor of Orissa, presently Member, Rajya Sabha, for the unceasing inspiration and affection he has showered on me and for the guidance I have received from him all throughout my humble endeavour to write on the life and philosophy of the great saint-poet Kabīr and for translating one hundred of his songs and equal number of *Dohās* into Oriya verse and then over three hundred of his *Dohās* into simple English rhymed verse, and subsequently for translating one hundred of his love songs into English in free verse style. He was kind enough to inaugurate the book of translation into Oriya verse of the songs and *Dohās* of Kabīr.

My gratitude to him knows no bounds.

2. I am beholden to Mr. Justice Ranganath Mishra, Chief Justice of the Supreme Court of India, for having gladly agreed to write the foreword to this book in spite of his heavy responsibilities as the seniormost Judge of the highest court of law in the country. Being deeply interested in the rich heritage of Indian culture, he has encouraged and inspired me to take up work on the Indian Epics and *Purāṇas* which I am currently engaged in.

I am highly obliged to him.

3. I express my deep sense of gratitude to the late Padmabhūṣaṇa Professor Dr. Ram Kumar Verma of Allahabad University fame not only for favouring me with an appreciation of this volume but also for the inspiration I have received from him but for which I would not have been able to do this.

4. I am very grateful to Professor J.M. Mohanty, Head of the Deptt. of English, Utkal University, Bhubaneswar for the enlightening Introduction he has favoured me with for this humble work. I have greatly benefited from the guidance I received from him in my translation of the couplets some of which bear the stamp of his able hand.

I am happy to record my heartfelt gratitude to him.

5. With a heavy heart I have to record my deep gratitude to my esteemed friend Sardar Santokh Singh of Bhubaneswar whose sad untimely demise has wiped out a loving and valued

friend. It was he who first inspired me to take up Kabīr, procured and supplied books on the saint-poet, and helped in the publication of the books. I owe the great departed soul a heavy debt of gratitude.

6. I record my sincere thanks to Dr. Shankarlal Purohit, Ex-Principal of Hindi Teaching Training Institute, Bhubaneswar for having helped me to comprehend the import of the *Dohās* and songs of Kabīr and in many other ways on my work on Kabīr.

7. I record with great pleasure my heartfelt thanks to my grand daughter Sarmistha Mohapatra, a student of Sri Venkateswara College, New Delhi and to my co-villager Shri B.P. Bhuyan, now in the employment of the Industrial Development Corporation of Orissa Ltd. Bhubaneswar for the help rendered by them ungrudgingly to make ready the manuscript in a neat and tidy manner.

8. Last but not least I am to record my sincere thanks to Mr. J.P. Jain, Director of the reputed House of Motilal Banarsidass Publishers Pvt. Ltd. of Delhi, the pioneers in the publication of standard books on Indology, to have agreed to take this up for publication.

G.N. DAS

Excerpts from appreciation by Padmashree Dr. Ram Kumar Verma of Allahabad University known scholar and writer on Kabir.

I am happy to record my appreciation to the translations of saint Kabir's dohas made by Shri Gananath Das in the simple and expressive way in which Kabir himself wrote them.

Kabir through his message for the welfare of humanity has become an international poet and the translation made by Mr. Das will be read and appreciated by readers in the West unfamiliar with Devanagari in which the poems are available.

I congratulate Shri Gananath Das for his remarkable work.

Lucknow

DR. RAM KUMAR VERMA

Couplets from Kabīr

ON GURUDEVA OR THE PRECEPTOR

[1]

कह कबीर गुरू एक सुधि बताई ।
सहज सुभाई मिले राम राई ॥

Says Kabīr, the wise preceptor
    Has given the know-how anon
To realise the Supreme Lord, Rāma,
    By simple practice of love-devotion.

Kabīr has declared unhesitatingly that it is his preceptor who gave him the know-how to realise the Supreme Lord Rāma. That know-how is to seek Him adopting simple practice of love-devotion.

And because the preceptor gave him the know-how to realise the Lord, Kabīr has proclaimed that if the preceptor and the Lord stand together he would first bow before the preceptor.

[2]

गुरू बिचारा क्या करे सबद न लागे अंग ।
कहे कबीर मैली गजी कैसे जागे रंग ॥

Says Kabīr,
If the preceptor's words enkindle not?
    He is not to blame
If the cloth is all full of *dirt*
    Can it take colour's flame?

Kabīr implies that the disciple must prepare his mind and heart to understand and imbibe the words of advice of the preceptor. He says that if a piece of cloth is dirty it cannot catch or retain the dye applied to it. But we cannot in that case find faults with the dye.

[3]

गुर धोबी सिख कपड़ा, साबू सिरजन हार ।
सुरति सिला पर धोइये, निकसैं ज्योति अपार ॥

Preceptor, the washerman, disciple, the cloth
    And Lord's Name the soap
On the washing stone of love
    It is washed to glow superb.

Kabir implies that the wise preceptor by imparting the Lord's
Name to the disciple and showering his love and blessing would
make the disciple as wise as himself. The preceptor would 'wash'
him clean as a washerman would a cloth.

[4]

पहिले दाता सिख भया, तन मन अरपा सीस ।
पांछे दाता गुर भया, नाम दिया बखसीस ॥

Disciple is the first to give
    He surrenders his mind, heart and head
The preceptor later gives his gift
    Of blessing, and Name of the Lord.

Between the disciple and the preceptor, the former is the first who
makes his gift to the preceptor by way of surrendering his body,
his desires and his thoughts. Later the preceptor makes his gift
of the Lord's Name and his blessings to the disciple.

[5]

गुर कुम्हार सिख कुंभ है, गढ़ गढ़ काढ़ै खोट ।
अंतर हात सहार दे, बाहर बाहै चोट ॥

Preceptor, the potter, disciple, the pot
    He cures the defects by cautious move
And protects with palm from inside
    As he beats it from above.

Kabīr likens the disciple to the unbaked earthen pot, and the preceptor to the potter who shapes it by removing its defects with beatings from above and protection from within. He implies that in the same way the preceptor protects his disciples during their trials and tribulations.

[6]

भेदी लिया साथ करि, दीन्हा बस्तु लखाय ।
कोटी जनम का पंथ था, पल में पहुँचा आय ॥

I took the knowledgeable one with me
Who showed me the Real Thing
What would have taken me million lives
In moments I saw the Supreme Being.

Kabīr implies that with the help of the wise and gracious precep-tor it was possible for him to gain the ultimate knowledge of the Lord, to acquire which it would have otherwise taken him not one but innumerable lives.

[7]

एक हमारी सीख सुन, जो तु हुआ सीख ।
करूं करूं तो क्या कहै, किया है तो दीख ॥

Listen to me my dear boy;
If you are my disciple
Do not just talk, 'you will do the job'
Do it and show your mettle.

The true preceptor wants from the disciple not merely a promise of following his instructions but a genuine fulfilment of that promise.

[8]

गुरू कीजिए जानिकैं, पानी पीवैं छानि ।
बिना बिचारै गुरू करें, परे चौरासी खानि ॥

Do select your preceptor with care
  As you skim your drinking water
If carelessly you select him
  You face the birth-death eddy, be sure.

Kabīr cautions that if one does not select his preceptor carefully he is bound to be misguided, and will miss salvation.

[9]

गुरू मिला जानिये, मिटे मोह तन ताप ।
हरस सोक ब्यापे नहीं, तब गुरू श्रापे श्राप ॥

If you get the right preceptor
  You overcome worries and attachment
Pleasure and pain you feel alike
  You gain your preceptor's bent.

If the right preceptor is selected carefully he endows the disciple
with his own qualities whereby the latter is able to shun attachment, and feel alike in both pleasure and pain.

[10]

सदगुर ऐसा कीजिये, लोभ मोह भ्रम नाहिं ।
दरिया सों न्यारा रहै, दीसै दरिया माहिं ॥

Make him your preceptor who has no greed
  And attachment and strife of mind
Though living on earth, is unattached
  To earthly ties that bind.

Kabīr advises that such a preceptor should be selected as is
above greed and is also above earthly bonds that bind man and
has no strife of mind.

[11]

भूठे गुर के पक्ष को, तजत न कीजें बार ।
ग्यान न पावै सबद का, भटकै बारंबार ॥

Tarry not to leave the preceptor
>Who deceives and misleads you
Cannot impart knowledge of scriptures
>You will wander and suffer too.

One should hasten to discard the so-called preceptor who deceives and misleads his disciple so that the disciple wanders in vain and suffers miseries.

ON 'IṢṬA DEVA' OR THE SUPREME LORD

[12]

पैठा है घट भीतर, बैठा है साचेत ।
जब जैसी गति चाहत, तब तैसी मति देत ॥

Sitting alert in every man
>Directs his action
In whichever way he wants to go
>Gives him that notion.

Kabīr asserts that the Creator remains concealed in every being created by Him as *Jīvātmā* or human soul, and indicates that He guides everyone according as the man wants by giving him that inclination and direction. Kabīr implies that as man has been specially endowed with intelligence, power of speech and thinking, and conscience to discriminate between good and bad, he should be able to beseech God for such help as would be good for him. This, indicates Kabīr, is the personal responsibility of every man in his own interest.

[13]

त्रादि हती सब त्राप मैं, सकल हती ता मांहि ।
ज्यों तरवर के बीज मैं, डार पात फल छाँहि ॥

God is the Source of the Universe
   He is all creation's root
Like seed of tree that holds the leaf
   The branch and the fruit!

Like the tree with its leaves, branches, fruits and flowers existing
in a dormant state inside the seed, all the creatures and everything on earth have their origin and source in the Lord.

[14]

तेरा सांइ तुझ में, ज्यूं पुहुपन में बास ।
कस्तूरी का मिरग ज्यों, फिर फिर ढूंढ़े घास ॥

Like fragrance in the heart of flower
   In you the Lord dwells
Musk is lodged in the navel of deer
   Like the deer you seek Him somewhere else.

Kabir points out that God dwells in the heart of man like fragrance in the flower and musk in the navel of the deer, but man
seeks Him elsewhere than his own heart like the deer seeking the
musk all over the forest instead of turning to his own navel.

[15]

अवगुण मेरे बापजी, बकस गरीब निवाज ।
जौं हौं पूत कपूत हौं, तऊ पिता को लाज ॥

Do rid me of my blemishes
   O my kind Father
I your son, if I am vicious,
   Is not the shame Your share?

God being father of all creatures, should be beseeched to help
remove the blemishes of the son as the shame of it is also His
share. This is a rare word of supplication to the Lord. Kabir

would ordinarily prefer to clean up his own heart by leading a righteous life. The Lord will then of his own accord shower His blessings on the devotee. This is what he affirms in Couplet 108.

[16]

ज्यों नैनो में पूतली, त्यों मालिक घट माहि ।
मूरख लोग न जानहिं, बाहर ढूंढ़न जाहिं ॥

The Lord dwells in the heart of men
    Like the pupil in the eye
Fools this wisdom never gain
    They seek Him far and nigh.

The Lord is in every creature like the pupil in the eye, but due to ignorance man does not realise this; he seeks Him everywhere else, points out Kabīr.

[17]

पुहुप माहि ज्यूं बास बसत है, मुकुर माहि जस छाइ ।
तैसे ही हरि बसें, निरंतर मेरे घट माहि ॥

As fragrance in the heart of flower
    As reflection in a mirror
Like that is the Lord staying always
    In my mind's bower.

The Lord dwells always in the mind of man like the perfume in the flower and the reflection in the mirror, indicates Kabīr. He implies that the Lord dwells in the mind of man in a subtle way in an unseen and unknown manner, and has been named *Jīvātmā*.

[18]

कबीर जंत्र न बाजइ, टूट गए सब तार ।
जंत्र बिचारा क्या करे, गए बजावण हार ॥

Says Kabīr, silent is the Veeṇā now
　　Its strings are snapped and gone
But what can the Veeṇā do and how?
　　Its player is no longer under the Sun.

It is the musician who plays the Veeṇā and if the strings of the
Veeṇā are snapped, and the musician is no more, nothing can be
done by the Veeṇā to revive itself. Kabīr implies that it is the
Lord who can make or unmake things and that man is as helpless and inert as the lifeless Veeṇā without the kindness of the
Lord who is the cosmic Musician and the universe runs to His
music.

[19]

जो मतवारे राम के, लगन होय मन माहिं ।
ज्यों दरपण की सुंदरी, किनहिं पकड़ा न जाहिं ॥

He who pines for the Lord in heart
　　He can see Him there
Like face in mirror He can be seen
　　None can catch Him anywhere.

If yearning for the Lord is earnest and determined in the heart,
one will be able to see Him face there but He can only be seen
like the reflection in the mirror which can be seen but not
caught, indicates Kabīr.

[20]

जाके मुंह माथा नहीं, नहीं रूप का रूप ।
पुहुप बास ते पतला, ऐसा तत अनूप ॥

The Lord hath neither head nor face
　　No body at all has He
Subtler far than flower's fragrance
　　Is His essence that be.

God has no body, face, mouth or shape and size of any kind, affirms Kabīr. In essence He is finer than even the perfume of the flower.

[21]

रहै निराला माँउ थे, सकल माँउ ता मांहि ।
कबीर सेवै तास कूं , दूजा कोउ नाहिं ॥

The entire cosmos is in Him
    Yet distinct and apart is He
Says Kabīr, he worships none other than Him
    The Supreme Power that be.

Kabīr says that he worships the Supreme God, the Supreme Power, in whom the entire cosmos dwells, yet He remains distinct from it. He indicates the position of the God-Head *vis-a-vis* the cosmos. The position becomes clearer when we turn our attention to verse no. 161. It is the decree of the Lord that runs the Universe. He remains the impersonal Supreme Power.

[22]

साहब तेरी साहबी, सब घट रह्या समाय ।
ज्यों मेंहदी के पात में, लाली लखा न जाय ॥

Unseen, unknown to everyone
    Is the red in 'Mehadī' foliage
So the Lord dwells in every being
    But beyond anybody's gaze.

Kabīr cites the common example of making the 'mehadī' leaves into paste and applying it to hand, feet etc. as girls do for imparting red tinge to them. Like the red in the green 'mehadī' leaf, the Lord dwells in every being unseen by all.

[23]

हांसी खेली हरि मिलें, तो कौन सहे सरसान ।
काम क्रोध तृष्णा तजें, ताहि मिलें भगवान ॥

If sporting and laughing you get the Lord
　　Why need you suffer pain?
No, if not desire, ire and lust bereft
　　Hope not the Lord to gain.

Kabīr indicates that one cannot get the Lord by taking it lightly
without suffering the pain of yearning for Him and without
abandoning lust, anger and greed from the heart.

[24]

साँई सूं सब होत है, बंदे से कछु नाहिं ।
राई थें परबत करे, परबत राई माहिं ॥

God Almighty can do it all
　　No man can ever do
Mountain He can make mole-hill
　　And mole-hill mountain too.

The Lord can make a mountain of the mole-hill and vice-versa
but no man can do this. Kabīr implies that man's abilities are
extremely limited, and he should always be conscious of his
limitations.

[25]

सात समंद मसी करौं, लेखनि सब बनराइ ।
धरती सब कागद करौं, तउ हरि गुन लिखन न जाइ ॥

With waters of the seven seas as ink
　　All trees of earth as pen
Whole of the earth surface as paper
　　God's merits cannot all be written.

Kabīr affirms that with the whole of the earth surface as paper, the entire ocean water as ink and all the trees in the forests as pen it will not be possible to write down all the merits of the Lord.

[26]

सब घट मेरा साँइयाँ, खाली घट नहीं कोय ।
बलिहारी वा घट की, जा घट परघट होय ॥

The Lord dwells in every being
    None is bereft of Him
Praise to him in whom He does
    Manifest His Beam.

The Lord dwells in every being without exception, but the man in whom He manifests Himself, i.e. the man in whom His presence is felt by others, that man is god-like. He is righteous and noble, worthy of all praise and respect.

ON 'PREMA BHAKTI' OR LOVE-DEVOTION FOR THE LORD.

[27]

सबै हमरे एक है, जो सुमिरे हरि नाम ।
बस्तु लही पहचान कँ, बासन सों क्या काम ॥

All who meditate on the Lord
    Are equal in my vision
It is the thing contained that matters
    Not the pot that did contain.

Kabīr asserts that all who are dedicated to the Lord and chant His name are equal in his view. Differences in their caste, creed, colour, language, etc. are of no consequence. It is the thing contained and not the shape or size of the container that really matters.

[28]

जब दिल मिला दयाल सों, तब कछु अंतर नाहि ।
पाला गलि पानी भया, ज्यों हरिजन हरि मांहि ॥

If the heart mingles in the Lord's
    There is complete union
As melting ice mingles in water
    In God the man of devotion.

If the devotee's heart reaches the Lord it mingles completely in
Him without maintaining any distinction. It is like melting of ice
and the water mingling in water. Kabīr implies that the union
of the soul of man (*Jīvātmā* and the Supreme Soul (*Paramātmā*)
makes them indistinguishable from each other after the union.

[29]

पहलो अंगन बिरह को, पाछे प्रेम को प्यास ।
कहे कबीर तब जानिये, नाम मिलन की आस ॥

The first step is pining for the Lord
    Next, craving for His love
Says Kabīr, then one may hope, my friend
    Love of the Lord to have.

Kabīr indicates the steps towards hopefully earning the love of
the Lord—first pining for the Lord and, next, earnestly craving
for His love.

[30]

जैसा ढूंढन मैं फिरूं, तैसा मिला न कोय ।
ततबेता तिरगुन रहित, निरगुन सों रत होय ॥

I could not find the one I sought
    Who is above the three '*Guṇas*'
Is wise, and for the formless God,
    Deep abiding love he has.

It is rare to find one who is proficient in spiritual wisdom, is above the three *Guṇas* (viz. *sattva*, *rajas*, and *tamas* or truth, materialism, and ignoble qualities) and also has for the formless God deep and abiding love.

Men ordinarily fall into one or the other of these three categories. Kabīr seeks one who has transcended them and has also deep love for the formless God. Such souls are rare to find.

[31]

ऐसा कोई ना मिला, जलती जोत बुझाय ।
कथा सुनाये नाम की, तन मन रहै समाय ॥

I have not so far seen the man
Who quenches burning fire
Brings message of the Lord's Name
That fills mind and body for ever.

Kabīr implies that it is rare to find a man who by his wisdom removes from another the anxieties and anguish of his mind and by reciting the Name and message of the Lord, fills the latter's mind and body with love and reverence for Him.

[32]

सारा सूर बहु मिलें, घायल मिला न कोय ।
घायल को घायल मिलें, राम भक्ति दृढ़ होय ॥

Met many a brave imposing man
Hurt and humble saw none
One himself hurt can find the others
Who have for the Lord strong devotion.

There are multitude men of brave and imposing nature, but meek and humble men are very rare. Kabīr asserts that only those who have deep and true love for the Lord are meek and humble and such men are rare, and only those who have deep and strong devotion for the Lord can find such rare souls.

[33]

तिन सनेही बहु मिले, चौथा मिला न कोय ।
सबहु पियारे राम कैं, बैठे परबस होय ॥

Many long for honour, wealth, and lust
    None for salvation
Those who do, they remain lost
    In His love and devotion.

It is only those few who remain completely lost in the love and devotion of the Lord, that crave for salvation. Most men on earth crave for wealth, power, and lust and have no craving for salvation. By '*tīna*' Kabīr implies the three powerful bonds of wealth, power and lust that bind men inextricably to the worldly ways.

[34]

कथ हो कथै सो पूत हमारा, पद गावै सो नाती ।
रहनी रहै सो गुर हमारा, हम रहनी के साथी ॥

Who talks of the Lord, is dear as son
    My grandson, who sings His glory,
The principled man is my preceptor
    I am principle's votary.

Kabīr implies that any one who talks or sings the praise of the Lord is dear to him as his son or grandson, and the one who follows the principles laid down by the scriptures is his preceptor and that he likes to befriend the man of principles.

[35]

जा घट प्रेम न संचरे, सो घट जानु मसान ।
जैसे खाल लुहार की, सांस लेतु बिन प्रान ॥

Where love of the Lord flourishes not
    That heart like 'Śmaśāna' is drear

It is like the mechanical breathing of
The blacksmith's lifeless blower.

According to Kabīr, the heart which does not harbour the Lord
with love is a dull and drear one like the cremation ground, and
it operates like the mechanical breathing of the lifeless blower
of the blacksmith.

[36]

पोथी पढ़ि पढ़ि जग मुश्रा, पंडित हुश्रा न कोय ।
ढाई अक्सर प्रेम का, पढ़ै सो पंडित होय ॥

Reading and reading all the scriptures
    None becomes a wise man
Knowing the two syllables 'Love'
    Makes you the wise one.

It is not by reading the scriptures again and again that one
becomes learned and wise, but by knowing the essence of love
of the Lord that one becomes learned and wise.

[37]

कांच कथीर अधीर नर, तीन्हे न उपजै प्रेम ।
कहै कबीर कसनी सहै, कै हीरा कं हेम ॥

The severity of the touch-stone test
    Can be withstood by diamond and gold,
Says Kabīr, glass like callous, and restless heart
    Cannot catch the Lord's love in its fold.

If the heart of a man is callous and hard it cannot catch the
Lord's love, says Kabīr. Only the touch-stone is capable of
registering the real quality of gold and diamond on it. Like that
the heart of a man should be pure and stainless. Only then does
it become capable of imbibing and retaining the love of the
Lord.

[38]

लौ लागी तो जानिये, छुटि न कबहूं जाय ।
जीवत लौ लागी रहै, मुये तहं समाय ॥

Firm love and devotion for the Lord
    Never leaves the heart
It stays till end and goes with soul
    From soul does not depart.

If once the love of the Lord and devotion for Him have taken
root in the heart of man they stay on. Even after death they go
along with the soul, do not ever depart from it, affirms Kabīr.

[39]

कुलबंता कोटिक मिलें, पंडित कोटि पचीस ।
सूद भक्त की पनहि मैं, तुलै न काहू सीस ॥

Many on earth claim noble descent
    Many more pundits claim knowledge
But none can compare to the devout's feet
    Though of lowly parentage.

A man may be of noble descent and great learning but he cannot
compare to the devout person although the latter may be of
humble descent, affirms Kabīr. In his view devotion to the Lord
scores much higher than caste or clan or even learning of a
person.

[40]

स्वांस स्वांस पै नाम लै, बिरथा सांस मत खोय ।
ना जानै उस स्वांस का, श्रावन होय न होय ॥

Chant the Lord's Name with every breath
    Waste not breath my dear
How can one at all be sure
    If the breath he will recover?

Kabīr warns that life being so uncertain not a single breath should be wasted without chanting the Name of the Lord for, he says, who knows whether the next breath will be vouchsafed to man or not.

[41]

कबीर रेख सिंदूर की, काजल दिया न जाय ।
नेनु रमाइया राम रह्या, दूजा कहं समाय ॥

Says Kabīr,
In the vermilion container
    'Kājal' one cannot keep
Lord Rāma resides in the eye
    None else can therein slip.

According to Kabīr, the Lord dwells in the eye as the pupil. None else can, therefore, be put therein at all as in the vermilion container one cannot put dark 'Kājal' or the eye-dye along with vermilion.

[42]

घटे बढ़े छिन एक में, सो तो प्रेम न होय ।
अघट प्रेम पिंजर बसें, प्रेम कहावें सोय ॥

Love that waxes and wanes in moments
    Is not true love as any can tell
Deep love that remains constant at heart
    That is true love that does not fail.

According to Kabīr, love that increases and decreases in moments without remaining constant and steady all the time in the heart is not true love at all.

[43]

कबिरा यह घर प्रेम का, खाला का घर नाहिं ।
सीस उतारे हाथ करि, सो पैसे घर मांहि ॥

Says Kabīr, this is love's abode dear
>   Not that of the aunt
Only he who can sever and offer his head
>   Can enter, others not.

Kabīr implies that the path of devotion for the Lord is the path of deep love, a path of continuous self-extinction; it is not a path for anyone and everyone, not as commonplace as the one to ones aunt's house. Only he who can sever and lay his head at His feet can have access to the Lord.

Elsewhere Kabīr has declared that devotion without love for the Lord has to be held as impertinence only.

[44]

क्या भरोसा देह का, बिनस जात छिन मांहि ।
सांस सांस सुमिरन करौ, और जतन कछु नांहि ॥

Can one rely on body-power
>   Which anytime death can smother?
With every breath take the Lord's Name
>   A better way there is none other.

Death can smother one any time, however young and strong. So Kabīr warns not to rely on physical power but to depend on the Lord and pray to Him for mercy and protection.

[45]

ज्यों लगि दिल पर दिल नहीं, लो लगि सुखहूं नांहि ।
चारो जुगन पुकारिया, तो संसा दिल मांहि ।

Happiness you can never find
>   Till you link your heart to His
And banish all the doubts of mind
>   True for all Ages is this.

Kabīr affirms that one cannot find true happiness till he links his heart to the Lord's, and banishes all the doubts of the mind on this score. This has been declared true for all the four Ages, *Satya, Tretā, Dvāpara* and *Kali.* The current Age is *Kali* or the Age of untruth and strife, according to the Hindu conception.

[46]

कबिरा भक्ति बगरिया, कंकर पथर होय ।
श्रंतर में बिस राखिकै, अमृत ढारि न खोय ॥

Says Kabīr, sans the Lord's devotion
　　Man is a piece of stone
His heart is full of bitter poison
　　No use pouring Nectar thereon.

Without devotion for the Lord man is no more than a piece of stone, and his heart is full of poison. Nectar poured thereon will be sheer waste. Kabīr implies that like any good seed thrown on infertile land, Nectar will go waste if administered to an un-worthy man.

[47]

मन प्रतीत न प्रेम रंग, ना इस तन में ढंग ।
क्या जाणे उस पीय सूं, कैसे रहसी रंग ॥

Deep and strong is not my love
　　Nor have I a beauteous face
I do not know my Beloved's ways
　　And if I can get His grace.

Proceeding on the path of love for the Lord, one feels uncertain as to how the Lord will take to him when he does not know His ways and does not possess anything special to attract the Lord. Kabīr wonders if the Lord would not mind his ignorance and lack of a charming face. He forgets for a moment that the Lord would like to see the qualities of his heart and not the charm of his face. It denotes his strong yearning for the Lord.

[48]

अकथ कहानी प्रेम की, कछु कही न जाय ।
गूंगे केरी सरकरा, बैठे मुसकराय ॥

Untold is the story of love
    Nobody can even guess
Like sugar taken by the dumb who smiles
    But its sweetness cannot express.

Love is something none can portray in words, says Kabir. The attempt would be as futile as the attempt to express the taste of sugar through a smile by the mute.

[49]

कबिरा बादल प्रेम का, हम पर बरस्या आइ ।
अंतर भीगो आतमा, हरी भइ बनराइ ॥

Says Kabir, love-clouds have gathered
    It is raining down on me,
My entire soul is soaked in it
    All round there is greenery!

Kabir, whose devotion for the Lord is dominated by love for Him, imagines love-clouds to be raining down on him from the skies, soaking his body and soul. He notices greenery all around. The rains of love have transformed him and the landscape around.

[50]

सबै रसाइण मैं किया, हरिसा और न कोइ ।
तिल इक घट में संचरे, तो सब कंचन होइ ॥

I have tried alchemy of all kinds
    Like the Lord's there is none other
In moments it spreads the whole body
    And transforms it to gold for ever.

After trying all kinds of alchemies, Kabīr has come to the firm
conclusion that none is as effective as that of reciting the Name
of the Lord. He implies that chanting the Lord's Name affects
the whole body in moments and man feels as if he had been
transformed into gold.

[51]

पासा पकड़या प्रेम का, सारी किया सरीर ।
सदगुरु दावा बताइया, खेलें दास कबीर ॥

Says Kabīr,
With the Lord's love as dice sticks
    And my body as the pawn
With preceptor's clue for moving it
    I play with confidence anon.

In one of the well-known love songs of Kabīr, the saint-poet
portrays the love game between the Supreme Soul (Paramātmā)
and the Soul of man (Jīvātmā) for ultimate union of the two.
There he says:

"I have staked my body and mind
    To play dice on wager with my Love,
If I lose, my Love wins me
    If I win, He becomes mine.
        *   *   *
In the game of dice
    This two-fold hope is always there.
        *   *   *
(translation by the same author: No. 71—awaiting
    publication.)

The above couplet is a pithy expression of the same feeling
where the craving for union with the Lord is expressed by the
saint-poet.

[52]

प्रेम पियाला जो पिया, सीस दछिणा देय ।
लोभी सीस न दें सके, नाम प्रेम का लेय ॥

Whoever craves the cup of Love
    Must lay head at His feet
The greedy man cannot do so
    Can only talk of it.

If one longs to drink from the cup of love of the Lord he must
sever and lay his head at the Lord's feet or, in other words,
completely surrender himself to Him. This calls for shaking off
greed from heart but one who is not able to do that may merely
talk of the cup of love, but cannot drink from it.

[53]

दुखिया मुंवा दुख को, सुखिया सुख को भूरि ।
सदा अनंदी राम को, जाकि सुख दुख है दूरि ॥

The sorrowful dies of his grief
    The happy pines and dies
The one plunged in the love of the Lord
    Neither grief nor glee he minds.

The sorrowful man wallows in his sorrow and dies, the happy
man pines for his happiness and dies, but he who is immersed in
the love of the Lord can be touched neither by sorrow nor by
happiness. He is not bothered about either.

[54]

प्रेमी ढूंढन मैं फिरूं, प्रेमी मिलै न कोइ ।
प्रेमी को प्रेमी मिलैं, तब सब अमृत होइ ॥

I searched for those who love the Lord
    But in vain, I found none;
Only one who loves can find the others
    And then Nectar will be born.

Kabir asserts that only he who loves the Lord deeply can find
the others who also love Him and when both will meet, nectar

will flow all around, viz., they will give the place a peaceful atmosphere.

[55]

स्वामी सेवक एक मत, मन ही में मिलि जाइ ।
चतुराई रीझैं नहीं, रीझे मनकी भाइ ॥

Master and servant thought alike,
    Being of single mind;
The Lord is not moved by cleverness,
    He wants one's love for Him to find.

The Lord does not notice any one's cleverness but is moved by the feeling of love in his heart for Him. Kabīr considers himself as the slave and the Lord as his Master. When man, the Lord's slave, is in deep love with the Lord both the Master and the slave become one or of single mind.

[56]

भगति दुहेली राम की, जैसी खांड़े की धार ।
जो डोले तो कटि पड़े, नहि तो उतरे पार ॥

Difficult is devotion's path to tread
    Like walking on a razor,
If you waver you fall on blade
    Or else you cross the bar.

Devotion's path is as difficult as walking on the blade of a razor. One has to do it very cautiously, or else he will fall on the razor blade and cut himself into two. If careful and steadfast, he will attain salvation to be sure.

[57]

कबीर माता नाम का, मद मतवाला नाहीं ।
नाम पियाला जो पिये, सो मतवाला नाहिं ॥

Says Kabīr,
He is drunk with Name potion
    And not with base wine
Who drinks the potion of the Lord's Name—
    With drunkards he is not in line.

One who drinks the potion of the Lord's Name becomes drunk with it and likes to drink more and more of it. But he cannot be classed with drunkards drunk with base wine, says Kabīr.

[58]

हमन है इस्क मस्ताना, हमन को होसियारी क्या ।
रहै अजाद या जग से, हमन दुनिया से यारी क्या ॥

I am mad with the love of the Lord,
    Why should I be careworn?
Not for me the lures of the world,
    I am attached to none.

Kabīr indicates that he who is mad with the love of the Lord is not careworn in any manner. He remains untouched by the lures of the world and unattached to any of the bonds of earth. One immersed in the love of the Lord is above worldly worries and allurements.

ON 'ĀTMA-SAMARPAṆA' OR SELF-
SURRENDER TO THE LORD

[59]

द्वार धनी कै पड़ि रहैं, धाका धनी का खाय ।
कबहुक धनी निबाजि है, जो द्वार छाड़ि न जाय ॥

At the door step of the rich,
    Though pushed, I shall sit;

One day or other He may relent
    His door step I will not quit.

By 'the rich' Kabīr implies the omnipotent Lord. In order to get
His mercy man has to surrender to Him with unflinching devotion in spite of inconveniences and never give up the effort to
gain His favour.

[60]

मुझ में इतनी सकति क्या, गाऊं गला पसार ।
बंदे का इतना क्या धन, पड़ा रहे दरबार ॥

What strength have I for serving Him?
    His glory can only quote.
What wealth have I to give to Him?
    Can only wait at His Court.

Man can do no more than sing the Lord's praise and work as
His slave. Kabīr implies that man's abilities and resources being
too limited he should always take refuge in the Lord.

[61]

कबीरा तेरी झोंपड़ी, गलकटियन के पास ।
जो करेगा सो भरेगा, तू क्यों होय उदास ॥

Says Kabīr, you have built your hut
    As neighbour to cut-throats;
But do not worry, for He who causes
    Will fulfil all your wants.

Kabīr implies that even if the neighbour is a cut-throat and
causes loss and misery, one should not worry because everything
happens at the instance of the Lord, and the loss or damage
sustained will be made good at His instance in due course. Men
need not, therefore, be perturbed for losses and gloat over gains.

[62]

जो है जाका भावता, जदि तदि मिलसी आइ ।
जा के तन मन सौंपिया, सो कबहुँ छाड़ि न जाइ ॥

One shall get what he aspires
    If ardent is his desire.
If to His will he surrenders,
    Can He forsake ever?

If one surrenders himself wholly to the Lord, all his desires get
fulfilled by His grace in due course, for He never forsakes His
devotees.

[63]

कबीरा पढ़िबा दूर करि, पुस्तक देहु बहाइ ।
बावन अकसर सोधि कै, ररै ममै चित लाइ ॥

Says Kabīr, give up reading books—
    Throw them into the stream;
One may just know the fifty two
    But concentrate on letters 'R' and 'M'.

It is no use reading and acquiring book knowledge. Books should
be thrown into the stream, says Kabīr. Only the letters 'R' and
'M' which make Rāma, the Presiding Deity, are all that need be
learnt, for 'Rāma' includes everything.

[64]

कंचन दिया करन ने, द्रोपदी दिया चीर ।
जो रीता सो पाइया, ऐसे कहै कबीर ॥

Says Kabīr,
The great Karṇa gifted his pelf,
    Draupadī tore her apron to give:
The Lord answered her anguished cry
    The humble does the Lord perceive.

Karṇa, the great hero of Mahābhārata fame was well-known for
his generosity. He gave away gold and jewels to any one who
begged. Draupadī, the consort of the Pāṇḍava princes, tore her
apron to tie up the wound in Śrī Kṛṣṇa's palm. The Lord
answered her call for mercy for He pays special attention to the
poor and humble and responds to their fervent call, asserts
Kabīr. Draupadī's call for help was at a time when she was in
great distress owing to the public disgrace she was subjected to.

[65]

कबीर किया कछु न होत है, अनकिया सब होय ।
जो किया कछु होत है, करता और कोय ॥

Nothing that happened was Kabīr's deed,
    What he did not did happen:
If anything happened that Kabīr did,
    Sure it was by some other done.

Kabīr is very emphatic in that everything happens according to
the will and direction of God, and so no one should claim that
he has done a thing, or undone another. He indicates the limita-
tion of man's resources, and abilities.

[66]

भूखा भूखा क्या करें, कहा सुनावै लोग ।
भाण्डा गाड़ जिन मुख दिया, सोइ पूरण जोग ॥

Why do you shout you are hungry,
    Is any one hearing you?
He who sustained in mother's womb
    He will feed you now.

God who sustains man in the mother's womb, will see that
he gets his food and no one else will hear if he shouts for food.
Kabīr implies that men on earth are selfish and callous to the
difficulties of others, and indicates that we should be sympathetic
and helpful to our fellowmen. (cf. Verse no. 95).

[67]

दूरि भया तो क्या भया, सिरदे नेड़ा होय ।
जब लगि सिर सोंपे नहीं, कारज सिधि न होय ॥

If you think you are far away,
    Surrender head—you will go near;
But if you cannot surrender,
    How can you succeed, my dear?

If one surrenders his head to the Lord, i.e. surrenders himself to Him fully, he will find that the Lord is quite near but otherwise He will continue to be far apart and unapproachable, affirms Kabīr.

[68]

भगति दुहेली राम की, नहिं कायर का काम ।
सीस उतारे हाथ करि सो लेसी हरि नाम ॥

Difficult is devotion's path
    It is not for the coward or tame;
If one can sever and offer his head
    Then he can take His Name.

Complete self-surrender is the only way to get realisation of the Lord and that is not an easy task, points out Kabīr repeatedly. The devotee has to be ready to sever and lay his head at His feet.

[69]

कबीर हीरा बणजिया, महंगे मोल अपार ।
हाड़ गला माटी गली, सिर सांटे व्यौहार ॥

Says Kabīr, precious is the Diamond,
    Its price is far too high,
Your bones and flesh will all wither
    And you lay your head to buy.

The Lord is the Diamond which sells very dear and even a whole
life time's effort may be inadequate. Only if one is able to sever
and lay his head at His feet, i.e. if one surrenders himself completely he may succeed to have the realisation of the Lord.

ON 'ĀCARAṆA' OR MAINTENANCE OF CONDUCT AND CHARACTER

[70]

हंसा बगुला एकसा, मानसरोवर माहिं ।
बगा ढूंढोरे मछरी, हंसा मोती खाहिं ॥

The crane and the swan appear alike,
    They feed from the same lake;
Crane hankers after fish alone,
    Swan prefers gems to take.

The swan and the crane appear alike while feeding in the same
lake but while the crane looks for fish and dirt the swan craves
for gems on which she feeds. Appearances are no indication of
one's nature.

[71]

ऐसा कोइ ना मिला, घर दे आपना जराय ।
पांच लरिके पटकि के, नाम में लौ लाय ॥

I could not find the man I sought
    Who set his house on fire,
Subdued his five naughty sons
    To meditate on the Sire.

Such men are rare as forsake attachment to home and family,
keep the five enemies (viz. lust, ire, greed, attachment and ego)
under control and deeply meditate on the Lord. Kabīr calls them
enemy's sons as they are man's constant companions like sons.

[72]

सीप ज्यूं तबलग उतरती, जब लग खाली पेट ।
उलटी सीप पैड़े गइ, भई स्वाति से भेंट ॥

Shell floats on its back in the sea
    Fasting for *svāti* rain,
As soon it drinks a drop of it
    It turns and sinks down fain.

The shell floats on the ocean waters on her back waiting for the
svāti rain with empty stomach, and as soon as she gets some
drops of that to drink, she conceives the gem, turns round and
sinks to the ocean bed with a contented heart. Kabīr implies that
in order to conceive and produce some precious thing one has
to put in determined effort like that of the shell.

[73]

पुहुपन केरी बास ज्यों, व्यापि रहै सब ठाँइ ।
बाहर कबहु न पाइये, पावै सन्तो माहिं ॥

Fragrance of the flower spreads
    Its sweetness in the air
None can see and catch it though
    You find it in the saint and seer.

One cannot see the perfume of the flower floating all around it
though it can be traced to the flower. Like that the tranquillity
of nobleness that one comes across occasionally cannot be seen
though it can be traced to the noble heart of the true saint.

[74]

तन थिर मन थिर बचन थिर, सुरत निरत थिर होय ।
कहै कबीर इस पलक को, कलप न पायो कोय ॥

Says Kabīr,
Whoever steadies his body, and mind
    And tongue, and conduct too,

Shall earn fathomless wealth of wisdom;
  None can gauge its value.

Whoever will be able to make his mind, body, word, character and conduct steady will gain the wealth of invaluable wisdom on earth.

[75]

पाप पुन्य की संका नहिं, स्वर्ग नरक नहिं जाहिं ।
कहत कबीर सुनहुरे संतो, जहाँ का तहाँ समाहिं ॥

I have no concern for heaven or hell
  Nor for piety nor sin;
Says Kabīr, O Saint! do let me tell
  I will be where I have been.

Kabīr says that he is not concerned with piety and sin nor has he fear of hell or lure for heaven; he is steady as and where he is. It is steadiness of mind and self-knowledge which take one far.

[76]

दीन गरीबी बन्दगी, सब सों आदर भाव ।
कहे कबीर सोइ बड़ा, जामे बड़ा सुभाव ॥

Says Kabīr, bow to the poor and humble:
  They are good to every one;
It is nobleness of mind and heart
  That is real greatness of man.

The poor is humble and good to one and all. They deserve to be given respect. Real greatness of man is goodness of his heart and conduct, and not his wealth.

[77]

ऐसा कोइ ना मिला, समझै सुने सुजान ।
ढोल दमामा ना सुने, सुरत बिहूना कान ॥

I could not find the wise man
　　Who listens with patience
But does not lend his mind at all
　　To trash and nonsense.

It is rare to find the really wise man who listens with patience to
all relevant matters, but does not lend his mind to irrelevant
matters. Kabīr implies that the man is rare who discriminates
between relevant and irrelevant, i.e. noble and ignoble matters
and does not lend his mind to the latter.

[78]

साध सती ओ सूरमा, इन पटतर कोइ नाहिं ।
अगम पंथ को पग धरें, गिरि तो कहाँ समाहिं ॥

The saint, the chaste woman, and the warrior
　　Are comparable to none;
They tread the hard unbeaten track
　　And when they fall, lo! completely undone.

None is comparable to the saint, the chaste woman and the
warrior for they follow a hard, unbeaten track, but if they fall
from that height it becomes completely ruinous for them, asserts
Kabīr.

[79]

दुख सुख दोनो एक समान है, हरष सोक नहिं ब्याप ।
उपकारी निहकामता, उपजै छोह न ताप ॥

Alike who is in his glee and gloom
　　Has banished all desire,
Of mirth and grief bereft helps all,
　　Is above pain and pleasure.

Kabīr asserts that one who has banished all his mind's desires
and is alike in glee and gloom and who helps others without any
self-interest, is above feeling of pain and pleasure.

[80]

कोइ एक पावै संत जन, जाके पांचू हाथि ।
जाके पांचू बस नहीं, ता हरि संग न साथि ॥

Rare is the saint, who has his five
    Sense-enemies controlled,
He can comprehend the Lord
    But not, if he has no hold.

Kabīr asserts that unless the sense-enemies of man (viz. lust, ire, greed, attachment and pride) are under control he cannot comprehend the Lord. He has repeatedly emphasised the importance of keeping the sense-enemies under control by the aspirant for success in his spiritual efforts.

[81]

बुरा न देखा बुरा न सुना, बुरा न कही जोइ ।
जो दिन खोया सब बुरा, मेरा बुरा न कोइ ॥

Who hears no evil nor does see
    Nor speak evil any more,
If he can cast all evil from him
    None will be evil to him here.

One who will not hear, see and speak anything evil and can cast away all evil from him none will be evil to him in life, proclaims Kabīr. So, one should be careful to eschew evil from himself.

[82]

सोना सज्जन साधु जन टूटे जुड़े सौ बार ।
दुर्जन कुंभ कुम्हार का एक धक्क दरार ॥

Noble man, gold, and wise saint
    Can rejoin again and again,
But the wicked, and the earthen pot
    Once broken cannot rejoin.

The scoundrel and the earthen pot once broken cannot rejoin though the saint, the wise man and gold can rejoin again and again. Kabīr implies that man should have a flexible and understanding mind to live peacefully in society.

[83]

गार अंगार क्रोध जल, निंदिया धुंत्रा होय ।
इन तीनों को परिहरै, साध कहावै सोय ॥

Harsh word is like burning coal,
  Sleep like smoke, anger fire
He who does these enemies desert
  Is true saint you be sure.

According to Kabīr harsh words are like burning coal, sleep like smoke and anger like fire. The real saint is he who has banished all the three from his heart.

[84]

कबीरा लोहा एक है, गढ़ने में है फेर ।
ताहिका बखतर बना, ताहिका समसेर ॥

Says Kabīr, from the same iron
  You make so many things:
You make the armour for protection,
  The sword for killing beings.

From the same iron, man makes the armour for protection and also the sword for killing. Kabīr implies that it is how man employs his resources of knowledge, intellect and bodily power, that matters, and that man should discriminate between good and bad to utilise his resources properly.

[85]

ऊंचे पानी ना टिकै, नीचे ही ठहराय ।
नीचा है सो भर पिये, ऊंचा प्यासा जाय ॥

Hilly places do not retain water,
    In plains it is plenty;
For water plainsmen do not suffer
    The hillmen remain thirsty.

Kabīr implies that humility is rewarding while uppishness or pride in man is harmful, and causes miseries to man as does scarcity of water to men living in high places.

[86]

कबीरा सोइ सूरमां, मनसूं माउं जूझा ।
पंच पयादा पाहिलै, दूर करै सब दूजा ॥

Says Kabīr, he is real hero
    Who has banished pride
Reduced the sense-enemies to naught
    And has no conflict of mind.

The real hero is he who has banished pride from mind and has kept under control his sense-enemies, (viz. ire, greed, attachment and pride) and has no conflict of mind. Kabīr implies that man has many enemies in himself and one who has conquered them is the real hero.

[87]

जो जस करिहै सो तस पाइहै राजा राम निआइ ।
जैसी कहै सो तैसी करे तरत बार न लागइ ॥

One shall reap as he will sow
    Is Lord Rāma's rule of law,
Sure salvation he shall gain
    Who acts as he does avow.

According to Kabīr God has laid down that one shall reap as he sows, and also if one acts as he professes he shall attain salvation without difficulty. If one indulges in evil deeds he can-

not evade the punishment due for that nor can anyone prevent
the rewards for his righteous deeds.

[88]

करताथा सो क्यों किया अब क्यों पछिताय ।
बोये पेड़ बबूर का, आम कहां से खाय ॥

Thoughtlessly you do a thing
　　　Then regret the result
If sour *Ambadā* tree you plant
　　　Can you get sweet mango fruit?

If knowingly one does a piece of thoughtless act, there is no
point in regretting the result which cannot be otherwise than the
inevitable outcome of the act. One should not expect sweet fruit
from a tree bearing sour fruits.

[89]

मानुस तेरा गुरा बड़ा, मांस न आवे काज ।
हाड़ न होत आभररा, त्वचा न बाजे बाज ॥

Character is man's only asset
　　　His flesh no use to any one,
His bone not fit for ornament
　　　And skin not fit for the drum.

Character is man's only asset, neither his bone nor skin nor flesh.
So, implies Kabīr, man should clean up his conduct, behaviour
and character. He attaches great importance to purity of character ranking it higher than even devotion for the Lord.

[90]

हरिया जारो कावड़ा, रस पारगी का नेह ।
सूका काठ न जारगइ, कबहु बूंदका मेह ॥

The living tree enjoys the rain
    It cools and feeds to fill,
The dead dry tree does not gain
    The cool of rain and thrill.

The living tree feels the cool of rain and feeds on it, but the dead
tree does not feel the thrill of it. Kabīr implies that man should
be alert to the blessing and gifts of God and be grateful to Him
for them and should not remain unfeeling and unresponsive to
His kindness.

[91]

कबीरा लहरी समद का, मोती बिखरे श्राइ ।
बगुला समा न जाएइ, हंस चुरो चुरि खाइ ॥

Says Kabīr,
Many gems are cast on shore
    By the waves of ocean,
They are relished by the swan
    Not noticed by the crane.

The waves of the sea scatter many gems on the shore. The swan
picks and eats them up but not the crane whose eye is on fish
only. Kabīr implies that depending on his innate nature man
chooses the good or the evil on earth, and gets results accord-
ingly. Also, because he has been endowed with intellect, wisdom
and conscience man should be able to rise above his innate nature
unlike animals who cannot do so.

[92]

सर्प ही दूध पिलाइये, सो ही बिष ह्वं जाय ।
ऐसा कोइ न मिला, श्राप ही बिष खाय ॥

Feed pure milk to venomous snake
    It will turn to poison;
None so far could I find here
    Eat and digest venom.

Pure milk turns to poison in the stomach of the venomous snake.
Kabīr implies that if one is evil by nature he will turn even a
good thing to evil but one who can turn evil to good is rare
indeed.

[93]

छिमा बड़न को चाहिये, छोटन को उतपात ।
कहाँ विष्णु को घट गयो, जो भृगु मारी लात ॥

Elders should pardon youngsters
    If they misbehave.
Did *Viṣṇu* suffer loss of prestige
    For the kick that 'Bhṛgu' gave?

To forgive the shortcomings of juniors is noble on the part of
their elders. Viṣṇu, the God Supreme, in Hindu mythology excus-
ed the kick that Bhṛgu, a saint, gave Him, the imprint of which
He bears on His chest. But that did not detract Viṣṇu's honoura-
ble position.

[94]

सातों सायर मैं फिरा, जंबू द्वीप दौ पीठ ।
निंद पराइ ना करै, सो कोइ बिरला दीठ ॥

I have crossed the seven seas,
    Visited countries many,
Nowhere could I see the man
    Who does not defame any.

There is none in the wide world, affirms Kabīr, who does not
defame any. Defaming others is a mean quality and man should
try to shun it. Elsewhere Kabīr has advised that one should not
be upset by defamation but give respect and honour to the
defamer as he (the defamer) cleanses one's behaviour and
character without any effort on one's own part.

[95]

यही पसु प्रबृत्ति है कि आपही सदा बरैं ।
ताही मनुष्य है जो मनुष्य लिए मरैं ॥

Animal nature is to live
    For selfish ends alone;
To die for others if need be
    As human nature is known.

Differentiating between animal and human nature, Kabīr affirms
that while the animal is self-centred, man should be ready to
sacrifice himself for others, if necessary.

[96]

घायल उपर घाव लै टोटे त्यागी सोय ।
भर जोवन में सीलवंत बिरला होय न होय ॥

Rare indeed are the men who bear
    Injury over their wound,
And those who endure loss sustained
    And in peak of youth are morally sound.

Those that can bear injury over wound and are not perturbed
over the loss sustained and also those who in the peak of their
youth are morally sound are indeed rare on earth.

[97]

चाह गइ चिंता मिटी, मनुवा बेपरवाह ।
जिन को कछु न चाहिये, सोइ साहनसाह ॥

If desire is killed, worries will go
    Mind will be carefree;
He who craves for nothing at all
    Sure king of kings is he.

According to Kabīr he who is able to banish all the desires of his mind will have no worries. He is really the king of kings for he does not have to depend on anybody for anything and as such is like a monarch subservient to none.

[98]

मैं मेरी सब जायगी, तब आवैगा और ।
जब यह निसचल होवेगा, तब आवैगा ठौर ॥

If you banish 'I' and 'mine'
    Steady will be your character;
If steadfast in mind, you will find
    You gain your life's anchor.

Kabīr indicates that by banishing selfishness man becomes steadfast in mind and character, and thereby he gains his life's anchor or shelter of the Lord that helps him to cross the sea of life and gain salvation.

[99]

दया कौन पर कीजिये, कापर निर्दय होय ।
सांई के सब जीव हैं, कीरी कुंजर दोय ॥

To whom shall one be merciful
    And to whom cruel?
All the beings are God's creation
    The insect, and elephant royal!

All creatures, big and small, on earth being the Lord's creation, one has to look upon them with equal feeling of love and compassion without any discrimination.

    In one of his songs known as *Love Songs of Kabīr* he sings as below:

*   *   *

I look upon all creatures of earth
Same as I may be
that I am sure will lead us on
to realise the Lord Supreme!

[100]

ऊँची जात पपीहरा, पिवै न नीचा नीर ।
कै सूरपति को जाँचइ, कै दुख सहै सरीर ॥

High is little *'papīhā's'* aim
    Would rather the pain of thirst suffer
Than drink other than rain drop water;
    But beg rain-god for early shower.

The little *'papīhā'* bird waits for rain water in spite of being
assailed by thirst and prays to the rain-god for early rain rather
than drink any other water. Kabīr implies that it is strong determination which would help man to achieve success in life and
that he should pitch his aim high.

[101]

देस देस हम बागिया, गांव गांव की खोरी ।
ऐसा जियरा ना मिला, जो लै फटकि पाछोरी ॥

In many a country and countryside
    Many a people I saw,
No where did I see the one
    Eager to scan and know.

Rare is the man who is eager to learn and who wants to test and
scan everything. Kabīr implies that to succeed in life, man should
be inquisitive and go into details and not be superficial.

ON MIND AND ITS CONTROL

[102]

मनहि दिया निज सब दिया, मन के संग सरीर ।
अब देवे को क्या रहा, यों कथि कहै कबीर ॥

Says Kabīr,

 If one has given his mind
  He has given his all;
 With the mind goes the body too;
  Then nothing remains withal.

Kabīr asserts that if one has given his mind to any he has given his body too, as with mind goes the body and the whole entity of man.

[103]

आपन पा मन अधीर भया सदगुरु दीनी धीर ।
कबीर हीरा बरणजिया मन सरोवर तीर ॥

Says Kabīr,

 Following the preceptor's advice
  I have steadied my mind
 And I now collect diamonds there
  Which I locate, and find.

Kabīr asserts that if one steadies his mind by following the preceptor's advice, he will get the best out of his mind which can go to the length of producing precious diamond. The word 'diamond' naturally has figurative suggestions.

[104]

भूप दुखी अवधूत दुखी, दुखी रंक बिपरीत ।
कहे कबीर ये सब दुखी, सुखी संत मन जीत ॥

Says Kabīr,
The king, the beggar, and the saint
  All are disconsolate;
Only he who controls his mind
  Is happy and content.

Only he who has full command over his mind can be happy and content at heart. All others beginning from the king to the beggar, who lack control over mind, are discontented.

[105]

पढ़ा सुना सीखा सभी, मिटी न संसे सूल ।
कहे कबीर कासे कहूं, यह सब दुख का मूल ॥

Reading and hearing all the scriptures,
  Learnt all the knowledge in them:
Yet doubts of mind did not go;
  Says Kabīr, from doubts sorrows stem!

The knowledge of all the scriptures acquired does not dispel the doubts of the mind. The doubts of mind being the source of all sorrows of man, steps should be taken to dispel them and make the mind stable by deep love-devotion to the Lord and by chanting His name, implies Kabīr.

[106]

सायर नाहीं सीप बिन, स्वाति बूंद भी नाहिं ।
कबीर मोती नीपजें, सुन्नि सिसिर गढ़ माहिं ॥

There is neither sea nor any shell,
  No 'Svāti' rain from the sky
Yet in the fort atop the hill
  Pearls grow, so does Kabīr say.

Kabīr indicates that without any sea or sea-shell and in the absence of *svāti* rain, gems are formed in the void space on the hill top. He implies that in the brain of the saints gems of spiritual experience are formed independently of any outward help.

[107]

दिल का मरहम ना मिला, जो मिला सो गरजी ।
कह कबीर आसमान फटा, क्या कर सके दरजी ॥

Says Kabīr,
> For my mind, I got no healing hand
> > But only men of selfish trend;
> If the limitless sky would burst and rend
> > How can a mere tailor mend?

For removing soreness of the mind heavenly aid is necessary as there is none around here on the earth to do that. Kabīr says that a mere tailor cannot mend a crack in the vast sky as that is beyond him. He implies that as for mending a rent in the vast sky the aid of heavenly hand or God is necessary, so for removing the soreness of the mind God's kindness is to be sought.

[108]

कबीर मन निर्मल भया, जैसा गंगा नीर ।
तव पाछी लग हरि फिरें, कहत कबीर कबीर ॥

Says Kabīr,
> I have cleansed my mind
> > Pure like Ganges water,
> The Lord now runs after me I find
> > Calling 'Kabīr' 'Kabīr'.

If one's mind is pure, God will run after him to shower all His blessings including salvation. Kabīr holds that purity of mind is more rewarding than even devotion to the Lord.

[109]

तन को जोगी सब करें, मन को करें न कोय ।
सहजैं सिधि पाइये, जो मन जोगी होय ॥

The ascetic dresses up his body,
    Mind he minds not;
That ascetic who trains his mind
    He succeeds in aught.

The ascetics dress their bodies only and neglect to train their minds. If they trained and trimmed their minds they would attain success in their efforts more easily.

[110]

बाजीगर का बांदरा, जीबा मन के साथ ।
नाना नाच नचाय करी, राखे अपना हाथ ॥

Like monkey of the magician
    Man is slave to mind;
It makes him dance to its tune
    And keeps him tied, you find.

Kabīr cites the popular simile of man being at the command of mind like the monkey in the hands of the magician, and dancing to his tune. He implies that for spiritual attainment mind has to be kept under control for mind being fickle is apt to mislead man and stand in the way of his spiritual progress.

[111]

मन पंछी तब लगि उड़ै, बिषय बासना मार्हि ।
ज्ञान बाज कै भपट मे, जब लग पड़े नार्हि ॥

Mind-bird flies here and there
    Tasting mundane pleasure,
As long as the knowledge-falcon
    Has not taken it over.

Kabīr likens mind to a bird roaming here and there after worldly pleasures till it is enlightened by the knowledge that these are all false and transitory. Man must, therefore, strive for this enlightenment.

[112]

मन के मारे बन गए, बन तजि बस्ती मार्हि ।
कह कबीर क्या कीजिये, यह मन ठहरे नार्हि ॥

One left for the forest for mind's fun
        Returned home at its bid again;
Says Kabir, but what else can be done?
        To waver mind is always fain.

Kabir has repeatedly laid stress on the control of the restless and
wavering mind and to make it steady; for achieving success in
any sphere a steady mind is essential.

[113]

कबीरा मन परबत हता, अब मैं पाया कानि ।
टांकी लागी सबद की, निकसि कंचन खानि ॥

Says Kabir,
Mind is like a lofty mountain
        Full of many a gem,
Getting the clue, I gained a mine of it
        Reciting the Lord's Name.

Mind can be productive of gems if man makes proper use of it.
Kabir says that he got the clue and chanting the Lord's names
he discovered a whole mine of gems in his mind. He emphasises
the great potentiality of the human mind for the uplift of man,
and implies that man should take advantage of this great
treasure.

[114]

कबीरा जोगी मनहि के, तन जोगी कोउ और ।
मन के जोग लगावत, दसा भई कछु और ॥

Says Kabir,
I am ascetic of the mind,
        Body I mind not;

If the ascetic would but mind his mind
    Different would be his lot.

Saints lose sight of their minds, and dress up their bodies to appear saints from outside. If instead they trained up their minds they would achieve success in no time in their spiritual efforts, indicates Kabīr.

[115]

तन सराय मन पाहरू, मनसा उतरी आय ।
कउ काहूका है नहीं, देखा ठोक बजाय ॥

The body is the guest house,
    Mind comes as guest there;
Know it for certain that the one
    Does not care for the other.

Kabīr points out that body is the guest house and that mind comes to it as a guest, but the mind and the body do not care for each other. He implies that there is no co-ordination between the mind and the body although they live together. This causes strife in the mind of man. Man should make every effort to maintain perfect understanding and co-ordination between them to avoid the strife.

[116]

मन दिया कहिं और ही, तन साधन के संग ।
कह कबीर कोरी गजी, कैसे लागे रंग ॥

Says Kabīr,
Here and there roams your mind
    With your body you strive.
Can unbleached cloth retain colour
    As much of it you give?

Mind being the motive force, if one does not apply his mind to the work that he is engaged in and does it mechanically with body effort alone he cannot achieve success. As a piece of cloth, which lacks clean texture, cannot take the colour of the dye, so will such a man not be able to achieve success in his effort.

[117]

जेती लहर समंद की तेती मन की दौर ।
सहजै हीरा नीपजे, जो मन श्रावै ठौर ॥

Countless are the waves of ocean
    So are waves of mind,
When waves abate and mind steadies
    Diamonds grow there to find.

Mind is as restless as the sea agitated by waves. But if one can control and make it steady it will be productive of priceless diamonds. As one can collect gems when the sea is calm, so can one collect diamonds when the mind is steadied.

ON 'MĀYĀ' OR ILLUSION

[118]

माया डोलै मोहिनी, बोलै मधुर बैन ।
कोई घायल ना मिलै, सांइ हिरदे सैन ॥

Māyā like a beauteous woman
    Tries to bewitch by her art,
But in whom the Lord manifests
    She cannot catch or hurt.

Kabīr expresses symbolically that *Māyā* or the bonds of earth try like a beauteous woman to bewitch and hurt man but they cannot harm one whose heart is illumined by the lusture of the Lord or on whom there is God's grace.

[119]

दीपक पाबक श्राणिया, तेल भी श्राणिया संग ।
तीनू मिल करि जोइया, उड़ि उड़ि पड़े पतंग ॥

The lamp brings oil wick and fire
    And lights a bright flame
It attracts all, its pull is dire
    Men jump in as game.

The illusions and attractions of the world allure man irresistibly
in several ways and he jumps headlong into the trap as insects
jump into the fire in the lamp and burn themselves. Kabīr implies
that men should guard against them by invoking God's grace.

ON 'CETABĀNI' OR WARNING

[120]

बिरिया बीती बल गया, श्रौ बुरा कमाया ।
हरि जनि छाड़ै हाथ थैं, दिन नेड़ा श्राया ॥

Gone is your youth, old age has come
    Yet you continue doing evil deed
End of your days is not far off
    Seek God's shelter, take heed.

The span of man's life on earth is a fleeting, short period. His
youth is soon overtaken by old age and then comes the end.
Kabīr warns that man should always remember God and seek
His refuge.

[121]

जो उग्या सो श्रांथिबै, फूल्या सो कुमिलाइ ।
जो चिणिया सो डहि पड़ै, जो श्राया सो जाइ ॥

> All that rises shall set one day
>> All that blooms decay
> What one builds shall crumble down
>> Whoever born shall die.

Kabīr indicates the transient nature of all earthly things citing many instances. He implies that man must remember this and not feel as if he has come to live for ever on earth and must, therefore, make earnest effort early in life to attain the goal of salvation.

[122]

ऐसा कोई ना मिला जासों कहूं दुख रोय ।
जासों कहिये भेद को, सो फिरि बैरी होय ।।

> I could not find the man in whom
>> I would confide my woe
> He in whom I did confide
>> Turned on me as my foe.

Such men are rare as would not turn the sorrows of others to their own account. Kabīr implies that confidants usually turn inimical and man should beware of them, and that instead of bewailing his lot before others he should take refuge in the Lord.

[123]

चिंता ऐसी डाकिनी, काटि कलेजा खाय ।
बैद बिचारा क्या करे, कहाँ तक दवा लगाय ।।

> Like a vermineus witch werry
>> Eats into your heart
> How can the doctor give relief
>> What remedy can he impart?

When worries eat into the vitals of man no doctor can treat him. Kabīr implies that worries should be kept at an arm's length, for they unsettle the mind, and that stands in the way of spiritual progress of man. Man should, therefore, ward them off by trying to concentrate on the Lord, and cultivating contentment.

[124]

जितना मैं किया तितना करि सकैं न कोय ।
काला मुखड़ा हो गया, धोय न सकूं रोय ॥

None other can commit all the sins
    Committed by me alone
All my tears could not cleanse
    Their stains from my face anon.

Tears of repentance cannot wash the stains of the sins committed by man. He can get purified of them only when he has paid for them, undergone the suffering they bring him or has atoned and made adequate amends for them.

[125]

भेष देख जनि भूलीये, बूझ लीजीये ग्यान ।
बिन कसौटी होत नहीं, कंचन की पहचान ॥

Do not judge a man by his clothes
    measure his knowledge
The real worth of the gold you can
    On the touch-stone alone gauge.

A man is not to be judged by his outward appearances. An ochre robe does not, cannot, make one a saint. It is his vision, his knowledge of truth and reality that make of him a sage. As you test the worth of gold on the touch-stone, so you measure the worth of a man by what he has come to know of truth and reality.

[126]

चातक सुतहि पढ़ावहि, ग्रान नीर नहिं लेय ।
मम कुल यही स्वभाव है, स्वाती बूंद चित देय ॥

Mother *cātaka* warns her fledgling
"Never you drink any water
Other than the *svāti* rain drop
That is our pledge my dear."

Mother *cātaka* (lark) instructs her tiny fledgling never to drink
any water other than the rain water that falls when the *svāti*
star is shining. That is their tribe's pledge. Kabīr implies that
one should honour the pledge, or tradition of the tribe or the
community or the family considering its value, and contribute
thereby to maintenance of community or social discipline.

[127]

तेरे हिय मैं राम है, ताहि न देखा जाय ।
दिल देहुरा के खबरि नहिं पाथर ते कह पाय ॥

Lord Rāma dwells in the heart of man
Him he never explores
Forgetting the God in the heart's temple
The stone idol he implores.

Man does not pay heed to the Lord dwelling in the temple of his
heart but goes on imploring the idol in the stone temple. Thus
does man waste away the human birth in a futile endeavour.

[128]

घर रखवारा बहिरा चिड़िया खाइ खेत ।
आधा परधा उबरै, चेत सके तो चेत ॥

The housekeeper is hard of hearing
Birds damage his crops
Do wake up and scare the birds away
And prevent further loss.

If the housekeeper is deaf, birds will damage the crops grown by
him without his knowledge. Kabīr implies that man being in

charge of his body and mind should not be unheeding to the words of his own wisdom, intellect and conscience with which he has been endowed by God. Otherwise he will be assailed by enemies, both internal and external.

[129]

कामी तरैं क्रोधी तरैं, लोभी की गति होय ।
सलील भक्त संसार मैं, तरत न देखा कोय ॥

The lustful, the greedy, the angry man
    Can atone for salvation
But for the liquor-addicted one
    There is no way to atone.

The lustful, angry and greedy persons can attain salvation but, says Kabīr, never the liquor-addict has attained it. In his view the liquor-addict is worse than the three other categories.

[130]

राजा की चोरी करैं, रहै रंक की ओट ।
कहै कबीर क्यूं ऊबरे, काल कठिन की चोट ॥

Says Kabīr,
How can any one escape
    The terrible doom of death
If stealing from the rich he seeks
    Shelter of the indigent?

Kabīr questions how one can escape doom if by stealing from the rich he seeks the shelter of the poor. Kabīr implies that he cannot atone for the sin of theft if he makes gift to the poor of what he steals from the rich. He has to suffer the outcome of the sin of theft.

[131]

लकड़ी कहै लुहार सुं, तू मत जारे मोहि ।
इक दिन ऐसा होयगा, मैं जारुंगी तोहि ॥

To the blacksmith the fire-wood says:
Brother, me you do not burn
Beware that day is sure to come
When it will be my turn!

The fire-wood warns the blacksmith to refrain from burning it as one day or other he will be burnt by the fire-wood. Kabīr implies that the dead body is consigned to the flames which are lit with fire-wood, and that man should be kind and considerate towards the poor and lowly for no body knows what latent ability they might possess.

[132]

माली ग्रावत देखि कै, कलियन कहैं पुकार ।
फूली फूली चुन लइ, कल हमारी बार ॥

Seeing the gardener in the garden
The buds wail to neighbour
"Full blown flowers he has taken
Tomorrow our turn dear!"

Seeing the gardener approach, the buds moan to their neighbours saying that he is plucking the full-blown flowers today; tomorrow will be our turn. Kabīr implies that man should be conscious of the transient nature of his life and seek refuge in the Lord.

[133]

कबिरा सोया क्या करे, जाग न जपै मुरारि ।
एक दिन है सोबना, लंबे पांव पसारि ॥

Says Kabīr,
No use sleeping inert
Not chanting Name of the Lord
Sure one day you will sleep for ever
Legs outstretched without a word.

It is no use sleeping and not chanting the Name of the Lord, cautions Kabīr, for one day or the other everyone will sleep inert with outstretched legs, on being overtaken by death.

[134]

दस द्वार का पींजरा, ता में पंछी पौन ।
रहै अचरज होत है, गये अचंम्बा कौन ॥

Ten are the doors to the cage
    There the life-bird stays
That it stays so long is strange
    Its flight should not amaze.

The body is like a ten doored cage in which stays the life-bird, the breath of life. It is rather strange that the bird stays so long without flying away, but its flight should not amaze. Kabīr stresses the uncertain spell of human life.

[135]

माटी कहै कुम्हार सूं तू क्या हंदे मोहि ।
एक दिन ऐसा होयगा, मैं हंदूंगी तोहि ॥

The soil warns and asks the potter
    "Do not knead me dear
Beware that day will come round sure
    When I shall knead you here."

The soil warns the potter saying that one day or the other the soil will knead the latter. So he should not knead the soil. Kabīr implies that when man dies he will be buried in the earth to become one with it. He also suggests that however lowly any object or creature on the earth may be, it has its utility. Man should take note of that and not harass the lowly and humble because of his weak position.

[136]

बिष के बन में घर किया, सर्प रहै लपटाइ ।
तासौ जियरा डरे रहता, जागत रैन विहाइ ॥

Your house is in the poison forest
    Where venomous snakes abound
You live in terror and unrest
    Awake all night round.

Man is bound to meet with result good or bad according as his deed is good or bad. If he selects a poisonous forest as his habitation he shall have to bear the consequences of his choice. Man should, therefore, be careful in all matters to avoid pitfalls.

[137]

नासमान जो बस्तु है, सो तो ठहरै नाहिं ।
तासों नेह न कीजिये, यह निस्चित मन माहिं ॥

All that is perishable shall wither,
    Of that you be sure;
Never be drawn to that at all
    Be firm in mind, do not waver.

Kabīr warns not to be lured by what is perishable on earth for one day or the other it shall decay and vanish. He implies that men should turn to God the eternal saviour for their salvation, and be not ensnared by the wiles of the world.

[138]

कहता हूं कह जाता हूं, कहा जु मान हमार ।
जाकै गल तुम काटि है, वह काटि गल तुम्हार ॥

Heed my words I tell you again
    It is he you want to maim,
Do try to get my word, friend,
    He cuts your throat to do the same.

Kabīr is firm in the conviction that if one does not want to harm
another the latter will not attempt to harm him. But if one does,
the other will attempt to do the same to him. Kabīr repeatedly
points out that man is bound to reap what he sows.

[139]

आया था किस काम को, सोया चादर तान ।
सुरत सम्हार ये गाफिला, अपने आप पहचान ॥

Why were you born on earth as human
    Why are you in slumber now?
Do take care of yourself man
    And try yourself to know.

According to Kabīr if, instead of leading a righteous life, man
indulges in indolence and slumber the chance of attaining salvation will slip from him. He implies that man should be up and
doing and make every effort for his salvation during his short life
span after taking stock of his real worth.

[140]

जब तूं आया जगत में, लोग हँसे तू रोय ।
ऐसी करनी ना करी, पाछे हँसे सब कोय ॥

When born on earth thou cried aloud,
    Others laughed in glee,
Do not in life do any such deed
    That they will laugh at thee!

Kabīr records the universal phenomenon of every child crying on
being born while all others present rejoice at the auspicious and
happy occasion. He warns that man should desist from doing
evil deeds in life. If man persiss in evil ways no one will shed a
tear on his death; it will come as a welcome relief to all he has
tortured with his evil deeds.

[141]

गंगा तीर जो घर करैं, पीबैं गंगा नीर ।
बिन हरि सुमिरन हरि ना, कह् गये दास कबीर ॥

Says Kabīr,
If you live near the Ganges
    Pure water you may drink
But sans His devotion and meditation
    You do not get the Lord you seek.

It is by single minded devotion and meditation of the Lord that
one may realise Him and not by observing formalities like living
on the sacred Ganges and drinking its water daily. Kabīr has no
respect for mechanical ceremonial rituals and piety. These cannot
purify man and prepare him for the vision of the Lord, his ultimate home, his last refuge.

[142]

खाय, पकाय लुटाय कै, कर लै अपना काम ।
चलती बिरिया रे नरा, संग न चलै छदाम ॥

Men eat, drink, make ill-gotten wealth
    Thinking they are clever
Beware when they depart from earth
    They carry nothing whatever.

Kabīr warns that man cannot take his hoarded wealth with him
after death. He should desist from making money by foul means
and hoarding it in the hope of taking it with him on departing
from earth.

    Man would forget his mortal lot, would sleep over it through
such fragile means as wealth and acquisitions. But these acquisitions cannot save him from his tragic lot.

[143]

मारग चलतें जो गिरा, ताकें नाहीं दोस ।
कहै कबीर बैठा रहै, ता सिर करड़े कोस ॥

Says Kabīr,
Do not take to task the man
    Who stumbles and falls in walking
But do whip him who sits in vain
    Lazy and idle without working.

Kabīr takes to task the man who sits idle and lazy and not the one who stumbles in walking. He denounces laziness in man. This is of course the surface meaning. But Kabīr is here referring to spiritual endeavour. He would like man to strive hard for his spiritual salvation even though failure may fall to his lot. Such a man will fare much better than one who does not, would not, strive and work for his salvation. The latter will have nothing but suffering for his portion.

[144]

आया है सो जायगा, राजा रंक फकीर ।
इक सिंघासन चढ़ि चलै, इक बंधे जंजीर ॥

All who are born—beggar, king or saint
    Sure one day will quit
One may be moving on his chariot
    The other with chained feet.

All who are born whether rich or poor shall die and depart from earth. Life is transient and no one can escape death. Kabīr has repeatedly warned about the transient nature of human life.

[145]

एक दिन ऐसा होयगा, कोउ काहूका नाहिं ।
घर की नारी को कहै, तन की नारी नाहिं ॥

One day it will happen so
    None will be there to look at you
Not to speak of your own spouse
    Your body will not be too.

No body on earth is selflessly attached to any one else, not even man's wife or, worse still, one's own body of which man takes so great a care all his life. On death the body separates from life, and drops down dead.

[146]

पहली बुरा कमाइ करि, बांधी बिष की पोट ।
कोटि करम फिल पलक में, ग्रायो हरि की ग्रोट ॥

All your life evil deeds you did
        A big bundle of that,
Hurriedly for good ones you make a bid
        To gain the Lord's support!

Man realises late that throughout life he did evil deeds and when he wants to retrace his steps to hurriedly do thousand good deeds he finds that it is too late and death is knocking at the door! Kabīr implies that man must engage in good deeds all his life without waiting till the last stage of life.

[147]

करम करीमा लिखि रह्या, ग्रब कछु लिखा न जाइ ।
मासा घटै न तिल बढ़ै, जो कोटिन करे उपाइ ॥

The kind God has written down
        The fate of every man
With all your effort you never can
        Change what He did ordain.

Kabīr implies that God writes down the fate of man according to his deeds and whatever effort man makes, it cannot be re-written either for the better or for the worse.

Man's life is the unfolding of his *prārabdha karma*, the deeds of his past life responsible for his present birth. No effort on his part can change the course of his life determined by his *prārabdha karma*. Man has to reap what he has sown.

[148]

कबीर हरि सबकूं भजैं, हरि कूं भजैं न कोइ ।
जब लगि श्रास सरीर की, तब लगि दास न होइ ॥

Says Kabīr,
The Lord thinks of all of us
    None thinks once of Him
So long we lean on ourselves
    To lean on Him we do not deem.

As long as man depends on his physical power he does not deem it worth while to seek the Lord's protection. By sleeping over the truth of his mortality man sinks in the ways of the world and forgets God, his true and sole refuge.

[149]

कबीरा बैरी सबल है, एक जीव रिपु पांच ।
अपने अपने स्वाद को, बहुत नचावै नाच ॥

Says Kabīr,
Powerful are the enemies five
    Of every single man
They do make him dance and dive
    In as many ways they can.

Kabīr warns that the sense-enemies of man are five in number, (e.g. lust, ego, ire, greed and attachment) and they overpower and make him skip and dance as they please. So man should be aware of these dangerous and fatal foes and should strive to thwart their evil designs.

[150]

बेरा बांधि न सर्प को, भबसागर के मांहि ।
छोड़ें तो बूड़त अहै, गहे तो डसिहै वांहि ॥

Do not build your raft with snakes
    The sea of life to cross
You shall drown if you leave the raft
    Or else be bitten by the venomous.

Kabīr indicates that if one takes a raft made of venomous snakes
to cross the sea of life he will simply be undone. Either the
snakes will bite him or, if he leaves the raft, the waves of the sea
will swallow him up. He implies that man should take refuge in
the Lord to cross the sea of life. Any other refuge will prove
treacherous.

[151]

काजर केरी कोठरी, ऐसा यह संसार ।
बलिहारी ता दास की, पैठिकै निकसन हार ॥

The world is like a vast room
    Of *Kājala* black in hue
Glory to him who enters here
    And goes unstained, such men are few.

The world is like a room full of black *kājala* (sticky substances
for anointing the eyes). Glory to him, says Kabīr, who enters the
room and comes out unstained. He implies that the man who can
live in the world unstained by sin and impurities is indeed a rare
soul.

[152]

पाव पलक की सुध नहीं, करे कल की साज ।
काल अचानक मारसी, ज्यों तीतर को बाज ॥

When one is not sure of the moment
    Why plan for the morrow?
Unawares death may strike him
    As does the kite the dove.

Kabīr cautions that death can smother one in moments. Yet man will not stop thinking and planning for the future. Kabīr implies that man should act in the living present without bothering for the future. He should leave the future in the safe hands of the Lord.

[153]

कुकुड़ी मारै बकरी मारै, हक हक कही बोलै ।
सबै जीव सांइ के प्यारै, उबरहुगे क्या बोलै ॥

Some kill the cock, others the goat
    They say it is all proper
To the Lord all creatures are dear
    To escape what excuse will they offer?

Some kill cocks and others goats for eating and both say that there is nothing wrong in it. All creatures being dear to the Creator, the Lord, they will have to explain their conduct before Him. What explanation will they offer before the Lord?

[154]

माखी गुड़ मैं गड़ि रही, पंख रहा लपटाय ।
तारी पीटे सिर धुनै, लालच बुरी बलाय ॥

The fly gets stuck in the molasses
    Get stuck its legs and wings
Pulled there by greed, the devil
    Its head and hands it beats.

Drawn by greed for molasses the fly gets stuck in it and cannot release itself from the sticky substance, says Kabīr. He implies that man should shun greed. Otherwise he will be in serious difficulty like the fly.

[155]

चित कपटी सब सों मिलें, मांही कुटिल कठोर ।
इक दुरजन इक आरसी, आगे पीछे और ॥

> The crooked man can mix with all
> But his heart is hard and gall
> Like the mirror the crooked man
> Within, without not same at all.

The crooked man has a sweet tongue and so can mix with all but, points out Kabīr, his heart is hard and evil. Like the mirror his exterior and interior are not of the same nature, he warns.

[156]

श्राव गया श्रादर गया, नैनके गया सनेह ।
यह तीनो तबही गये, जबही कहा कछू देह ॥

> Words of love and welcome dry up
> In moments and for ever
> As soon as you stretch your hand
> And beg for the smallest favour.

It is not advisable to beg even the smallest favour. That leads to the drying up of all affection and love.

Kabīr warns that man should desist from the habit of asking favours, often undue favours, which ultimately results in the loss of every sympathy for him for all time. This is a matter of common experience.

[157]

पल में परलय बीतिया, लोगन लगी तमारि ।
श्रागिल सोच बिचारिकैं, पाछै करो गोहारि ॥

> In moments deluge may over-run earth
> Yet man is wild in his pursuit
> Take stock of your position, man,
> Then you may press your suit.

The world may be over-run by deluge in moments. Even then men engage in petty selfish matters. They should take stock of

their future rather than steep themselves in selfishness. When they
have purified themselves of their selfishness they may then think
of their personal matter.

[158]

बिष का बिरवा घर किया, रहा सर्प लपटाय ।
ताते जियरे डर भया, जागत रैन बिहाय ॥

You have built your cottage dear
　　　Under the poison-tree
Venomous snakes cling to it
　　　You are never asleep, or fear-free.

Results follow action. If a man builds his house in a poison forest
where venomous snakes cling to the trees all around he cannot
have sleep at night for fear of the snakes and cannot ever remain
free from fear. Kabīr warns that man cannot avoid the consequences of his deeds.

[159]

सेमर केरी सूबना, सिहुले बैठा जाय ।
चोंच चहारें सिर धुनै, यह वाही को भाय ॥

The foolish parrot put her beak
　　　Into the red *semira* bud
Beak got stuck in its fibrous stock
　　　She got what she deserved.

Being attracted by the red of the *semira* bud the little parrot put
her beak into it, but it got stuck in the fibrous interior of the
bud. She mistook it for some luscious fruit and put her beak out
of greed and suffered the consequence. Kabīr implies that man
should shun greed which is one of his five powerful sense-
enemies; otherwise he would suffer as did the parrot.

[160]

नौ मन दूध बटोरि कं टिपका दिया बिनास ।
दूध फाटि कांजी भया, हुआ घिउ का नास ॥

Nine maunds of pure milk
    A drop of acid can spoil
The milk splits and its essence fat
    Is lost how much you toil!

A large quantity of pure milk can be spoiled by a drop of acid.
Kabīr implies that the life long record of good and noble deeds
of a man can be marred by a little evil deed. One should, therefore, be ever watchful and resist every temptation.

[161]

घाट भुलाना बाट बिन, मेस भुलाना कानी ।
जाकी मांड़ी जगत मां, सो न परा पहिचानी ॥

One may fail to reach the quay
    For not knowing the way
Beguiled by the dress of the man
    He may fail to know the guy.
But how can he fail to know the Lord
    Whose decree runs the world?

It is possible for one to fail to reach the landing place for not
knowing the way to it, and for mistaking a person's abilities
from his dress, but Kabīr wonders how he will fail to know the
Lord who rules the entire universe, and when the proof thereof
is all around!

[162]

कबीरा सांइ मुझ को, रुखी रोटी देय ।
चुपड़ी मांगत मैं डरु, रुखी छीन न लेय ॥

Says Kabīr

Let me have my dry bread, Lord,
Let me not covet *cupadī*
Lest, I should lose my dry bread
And for that be sorry.

Kabīr implores the Lord to continue to grant him the dry *capātī* which is his usual humble fare and says that he is afraid of asking for a richer fare lest he should lose thereby his humble fare of dry *capātīs*. He implies that man should desist from the temptation for richer food to satisfy his palate, and, for that matter, from all temptations for leading a richer worldly life.

[163]

बकरी पात खात है, ताकी माढ़ी खाल ।
जो बकरी को खात है, ताको कोन हवाल ॥

Just for eating leaves and grass
The poor goat suffers flaying
What help is there for the man who eats
The goat's flesh by slaying?

For mere eating of leaves and grass the goat gets the punishment of flaying, says Kabīr, and asks what help can there be for man for killing and eating the flesh of a goat? He implies that just for the sake of satisfying the tongue one should not indulge in killing of animals, birds, etc.

[164]

तकत तकावत तकि रहै, सकै न बोझा मारि ।
सबै तीर खाली परैं, चले कमानी डारि ॥

We waste our time in mere search
And fail to hit the mark
Then leave at last like the archer
Spending all his arrow stock.

Kabīr says that since the mind is not steady and set on a purpose man wastes his time searching for the target and so misses to hit it and at last leaves like the archer having emptied his quiver in vain. He implies that the mind should be steadied before one takes up an endeavour, and it should be set on the task.

[165]

दया भाव हिरदे नहीं, ग्यान कथै बेहद ।
ते नर नर नाहीं जाहिंगे सुनि सुनि साखी सबद ॥

He who has no mercy at heart
　　May cite the scriptures well
But he cannot at all be called a man
　　And for his own salvation fail.

One who has no mercy at heart may know and cite the scriptures well, but cannot attain his own salvation just for knowing the scriptures, affirms Kabīr. In Kabīr's view love-devotion for the Lord and purity of thought, deeds, and words of mouth score much higher than mere knowledge of scriptures.

ON 'VYAṄGA' OR SARCASTIC UTTERANCES

[166]

मूरख जन समभै नहीं, हित अनहित को काज ।
चूहा बिल घुसै नहीं, पूंछ में बंधे छाज ॥

What is good and what is bad
　　Fools cannot see at all
With a garment tied to its tail
　　Can the rat enter its hole?

Kabīr says that foolish people cannot discriminate between good and evil. Such men cannot reach their goal because the load of evil gets too heavy for them. Their fate is like that of a rat which has its tail tied up to a piece of linen. It will get too bulky for the rats' hole. He also implies that without comprehending the essence of things one cannot reach the goal of god-realisation.

[167]

जनमते मानुस होत सब, यह जानत संसार ।
बंचक सूद करावही, कहै कबीर पुकार ॥

Says Kabīr,
  All are born as human
    That is what all know
  The cunning deceptor has made some *sūda*
    Devising castes high and low.

It is well-known that all are born as human beings. The deceptors have devised castes high and low and divided men into high caste Brahmin and low caste *sūda* or *śūdra* etc. Kabīr was vehemently opposed to the caste system which has the effect of dividing men into opposing camps.

[168]

आये एकही देस थे, उतरे एकही घाट ।
हवा लागी जू संसार की, हो गए बारह बाट ॥

We all hail from the same land
  And reach here on earth
  Touched by the winds that blow here
    Each pursues his own path.

All men come from the same land, and reach earth as such, but the winds of the earth make them follow different paths. Kabīr implies that the origin of all human beings is the same viz. heaven, but after they are born on earth, they get influenced by the ways of the world. These ways divide them from each other leading them to follow divergent paths.

[169]

श्रासन मारे क्या भया, गई न मन की श्रास ।
ज्यों तेली के बैल को, घर ही कोस पचास ॥

What if one perfects *Yogāsana*
          Has not attained mind's desire
Like the bullock of the oilman
          Though near home thinks it far.

If man is devoid of longing for God-realisation, his proficiency
in yogic exercises will be of no avail. Like the bullock yoked to
the oil mill one will be in haze and not be able to see the actual
state of things. Kabīr implies that realisation of God is of prime
importance. Mere attainment of success in yogic exercise is of no
avail to him. He will continue to remain in haze like the bullock
of the oil mill.

[170]

श्रातम बुधि जानै नर्हि, न्हावै प्रातः काल ।
लोक लाज लियें रहे, लगा भसम कपाल ॥

Without knowledge of the self
          Man fears derision of others
Bathes and puts the ash on forehead
          To know himself never bothers.

Kabīr implies that for fear of others' derision man indulges in
outward shows like bathing at dawn, smearing *vibhūti* or ash on
forehead without bothering to understand the real import of self-
knowledge viz, that God dwells in him.

[171]

जप तप दीखौ थोथरा, तीरथ ब्रत बिस्वास ।
सूवां सेमल सोइया, ज्यों जग चला निरास ॥

For mere show the ignorant man
>Worships and visits sacred place
Like parrot tasting the *semira* bud
>Returning with disappointed face.

Kabīr implies that offerings of worship in the temple and visiting sacred places are of no avail to man. He courts only disappointment like the parrot tasting the *semira* bud and getting stuck in its fibrous structure.

[172]

कबीर ब्यास कथा करै, भीतर भेदें नाहीं ।
औरों को परमोधता, गये मुहर कमाहीं ॥

Says Kabīr,
>The pundit learned in scriptures
>>Can deliver talks of advice
>The words do never touch his heart
>>For others he does it for a price.

One who is well versed in the scriptures can deliver learned lectures on them, but if the words do not touch his heart he will not benefit himself at all by them. He delivers lectures for mere mercinary considerations.

[173]

अकील बिहूना सिंह जों, गए ससा के संग ।
अपनी प्रतिमा देखिकै, खोया तन के भंग ॥

Powerful though the foolish lion
>Duped by the cunning rabbit
Went to the well and jumped inside
>And lost his life in it.

Kabīr refers to a fable in which a rabbit lures a lion to a well. This lion was befooled into believing that another lion in the

well—actually his own reflection—challenged his supremacy.
The lion in his fury jumped into the well and was drowned. Kabīr
implies that it is intelligence and wit which triumph over physical
power and also that man should shed off anger, which clouds
his wit and intelligence.

[174]

तारा मंडल बसि करि, ससि बड़ाइ खाइ ।
उदे भया जब सूरका, ज्यूं तारा छिप जाइ ॥

In the sky at night the moon
    Out-shines the stars
At dawn as soon rises the sun
    Like stars she disappears.

The moon dominates over the stars in the sky at night but as
soon as the sun's rays come with dawn she pales and vanishes
from sight. Kabīr implies that man should be aware of his real
position, and should not be dazzled by temporary prosperity. He
should strive for real knowledge and not pseudo-knowledge as
the latter is of no value, and it pales before real knowledge as the
moon does before the sun.

[175]

हिन्दु मुए राम कहि, मुसलमान खुदाय ।
कबीर कहै सो जीबता, दुहूँ कहा न जाय ॥

Says Kabīr,
At death Hindus chant name of Rāma
    Muslims chant Khudā's name
In their life-time neither of them
    Does ever chant the same.

Hindus chant the name of Lord Rāma, and Muslims that of
Khudā at death, but during their lifetime Hindus and Muslims
do not remember to chant God's names or realise Him. Kabīr
derides the practice of ceremonial chantings at the time of

funeral. Those who would not spare time to remember the Lord in their lifetime cannot derive any good out of this ceremonial chanting.

[176]

बूड़ा बंस कबीर का, उपजिया पूत कमाल ।
हरि का सुमिरन छोड़ के, घर को लाया माल ॥

Says Kabīr I begat a son
    Kamāl I gave him name
This son grew up gave up meditation
    He ran after money and fame
I thought my progeny I was saving
    But way to its fall he was paving!

Kabīr implies that it is not at all desirable to run after wealth giving up meditation of the Lord. He is unhappy that his own son has been lured by wealth to forget the name of the Lord.

[177]

सती पुकारे सूली चढ़ी, सुनरे मीत मसान ।
लोग बटाउ चलि गए, हम तुम रहे निदान ॥

From her husband's funeral pyre
    The *sati* calls the funeral ground
"All who came have left us here
    You and I are only around."

Kabīr implies that after death there is none save the Lord who would care for the departed soul, citing that all those who came with the funeral procession have left and did not care for even the wife of the deceased whom they made to immolate herself on her late husband's pyre.

[178]

हौं तोहि पूछ्छों हौं सखी, जीवत क्यूं न मराइ ।
मुबा पीछ्छे सत करैं, जीवत क्यू न कराइ ॥

O, friend, why did not you *sati* me
  When my husband was alive
If you can kill me after he died
  Why not when he was in life?

The one forced to burn herself on the funeral pyre of her dead husband asks why she was not made *sati* while her husband was alive? Kabīr did not favour the practice of *sati* as it is clear from this and the preceding verse.

[179]

ऐसी गति संसार की, ज्यो गारड़ को ठाठ ।
एक पड़ा जेहि गाड़ में, सबै जाहि तेहि बाट ॥

Sheep-like behave all men on earth
  If one falls in a pit
All others go the self-same path
  And fall at last in it.

Men behave like sheep on earth and thoughtlessly they follow the lead of one and fall in the same pit into which he fell. Kabīr implies that men behave thoughtlessly on earth, blind to the consequences of their deeds and also that man should not blindly follow an ignorant preceptor for that would not lead him to fruitful realisation of God.

[180]

बामन से गदाहा भला, आन जात से कूता ।
मुल्ला से मुरगा भला, रात जगावैं सूता ॥

The donkey is far better than Brahmin
  Dog is better than other castes

The cock is better than the Mullah
They wake the people by their blasts.

Kabīr implies that dividing men into castes, clans and creeds renders no help to them; rather they engage in quarrels and feuds on that score. Better than the castes are, according to Kabīr, the birds and animals like the cock, the ass and the dog who render useful service to men by waking them from sleep in the morning.

[181]

करनी बिन कथनी कथैं, अज्ञानी दिन रात ।
कूकर ज्यूं भूकत फिरैं, सुनी सुनायी बात ॥

Who does nothing but talks too much
Being insensate and tense
Like the wild dog he barks always
Prattling words of little sense.

Kabīr decries the man who instead of engaging himself in some good or productive deed remains busy in talking. Such a man barks away his life like a wild dog.

[182]

बिन वासीलै चाकरी, बिन बुद्धि की देह ।
बिना ज्ञान का जोगना, फिरैं लगाये खेह ॥

Like service without salary
And body without intellect
The ascetic without wisdom roams
His body ash bedecked.

With ash smeared on his body, a so-called saint, without wisdom and spiritual knowledge, is like a service-holder without salary and a man without intellect. It is the internal realisation and not outside appearance which matters, Kabīr implies.

[183]

नवन नवन बहु श्रंतरा, नवन नवन बहु बान ।
ऐ तीनों बहुतै नबं, चीता चोर कमान ॥

Between humbleness and bowing down
    There is a lot of difference
The three, hunter, leopard and the thief
    Bow down much in excess.

Kabir points out that bowing down is not the same thing as
humility. He cites the case of the hunter, the leopard and the
thief who bow down too much but with evil intention. He implies
that one should beware of such people.

ON 'MṚTYU' OR DEATH

[184]

जैसा कोरी रेजा बुनै, नीरा श्रावै छौर ।
ऐसा लेखा मीच का, दौर सकै तो दौर ॥

The weaver weaving thread by thread
    Brings the end near
So death leads us step by step
    Run if you can run far.

Death is ever weaving its wide spread net to entangle creatures in
it. Let every mortal attain his end before death spreads its trap
for him. Kabir implies that in view of the uncertainty of human
life man should not indulge in indolence but be up and doing
always as death may smother him any time.

[185]

सांझ पड़ी दिन ढल गया, बाघिन घेरी गाय ।
गाय बिचारी न मरी, बाघिन न भूखी जाय ॥

Evening shadows darken deep
> The tiger prowls for the cow
He cannot kill the cow at all
> Hungry he cannot go.

The cow stands for the living soul (jīvātmā) which is eternal and does not die. Death, for which the tiger is the symbol, cannot kill the soul. The tiger will not, however, remain starved. It will kill the body. The soul which is attached to the body will bear the torture and agony of the death of the body. That is the price it will have to pay for its attachment to the body. The comments under verse 274 may be seen in this connection.

[186]

कबीर गर्वं न कीजिये, काल गहे कर केस ।
ना जानें कित मारि है, क्या देस क्या परदेस ॥

Says Kabīr,
Never be proud
> Death has thee in his clutch
Sure some day he will smother thee
> At home or not as much.

Kabīr cautions saying that man is always in the clutches of death and none can say when and where death will smother him. So, none should be arrogant.

[187]

पात भरन्ता देखी के हँसत कृपालिया ।
हम चली तुम चालिहै, धौरी बापुलिया ॥

At the falling dry old leaf
> The tender leaf does sneer
Says the falling leaf—
> "Today my turn, tomorrow yours
Have patience, O my dear!"

Kabīr implies that the same end, i.e. death, awaits all, some sooner and others later and so one has to be patient without sneering at another who passes away earlier.

[188]

तंसे ध्यान धरहु जिन, बहुरि न धरना ।
ऐसेहि मरहु की बहुरि न मरना ॥

Do so meditate on the Lord
    The flow of it will not drain
Do die that death O, my friend,
    You shall not die again.

Kabīr exhorts that meditation on the Lord should be deep and continuous and also that the aspirant should so strive that he attains salvation in life time and avoids rebirth.

[189]

कबीर संसा दूरि करि, जामरण मरण भरम ।
पंच तत्त तत्त ही मिलै, सुरत समाना मन ॥

Says Kabīr,
    You discard soon from mind
        The doubts of birth-death discord
The body mingles in the elements
        And mind in the Lord.

There should not be any conflict of mind regarding the problem of life and death, says Kabīr. On death the body mingles in the five elements of which it is composed, and the mind mingles in the Lord. Where man does not attain salvation, the mind with the soul (jīvātmā) has successive rebirths. This recurring cycle of birth and death will not stop until the mind and the soul mingle in the Lord on attaining salvation.

[190]

काल काल सब कोइ कहैं, काल न चीन्हे कोय ।
जेती मन की कलपना, काल कहाबे सोय ॥

All are talking of demise
  Not knowing what it is
The longings and desires of the mind
  Demise stems from these.

People do not know the real meaning of death which, according to Kabīr, stems from the worldly longings and urges of man. He implies that the longings and desires lead man step by step to old age and death, and also that he who can shed his longings and urges of mind becomes deathless by attaining salvation.

[191]

पात पड़ेता यों कहे, सुनि तरबर बनराइ ।
अब के बिछड़े ना मिले, कहि दूर पड़ेंगे जाइ ॥

The falling leaf says to the tree
  "Listen, O tree, to me
How can I rejoin the foliage
  Far from you shall I be."

The leaf once dislodged from the branch never rejoins it. Such is the fate of man. Once he dies it is the end of the human body once and for all. It does not revive after death.

[192]

कबीर पंच पखेरुवा, राखे पोस लगाइ ।
एक जु आयी पारधी, ले गयी सब उड़ाइ ॥

Says Kabīr,
Five little birds did I rear
  With tender care and delight

A wily hunter came one day
    And made them leave by flight.

Kabīr implies that man lives with his five sense-enemies (viz.
lust, ire, greed, attachment and pride) unconscious of the harm
caused by them. They persist in him till death. Kabīr indicates
that it is very hard to get rid of these enemies. By wily hunter
Kabīr means death. Only death puts an end to them.

[193]

यहु जीव आया दूर थे, आजौ भी जासी दूरी ।
बीच के बासें रमि रह्या, काल रहा सर पूरी ॥

Man has come from his far off home
    He still has to go further
Midway as guest does he stay and roam
    With death in ambush here.

According to Kabīr man hails from that far off land which some
call Heaven and has ultimately to go back there after his sojourn
on earth and after earning his salvation for the union of his soul
(Jīvātmā) with the Supreme Soul (Paramātmā). While on earth
death stands guard throughout, ready to smother him any time.

[194]

कांची काया मन अथिर, थिर थिर काम करन्त ।
ज्यूं ज्यूं नर निधड़क फिरै, त्यूं त्यूं काल हसन्त ॥

Old and weak of body and mind
    Man struggles and works
If ever he moves carefree
    At him death jeers and laughs.

Death is always watchful of man. When he finds man struggling
in spite of age and debility he keeps quiet. If he finds him agile
and active and moving briskly and carefree, he sneers at him.

The meaning is that death can smother him any moment in spite of his agility. Kabīr implies that man should not be forgetful of his ultimate fate of death.

[195]

कबिरा मैं तो तब ड़रों, जो मुभ ही मैं होय ।
मीच बुढ़ापा ग्रापदा, सब काहु में सोय ॥

Says Kabīr,
I would fear death, dotage, and danger
  Were they for me alone
But every creature suffers all that
  Why shall I be terror-worn?

Kabīr says that because calamity, old age and death are universal phenomena and happen to all, he is not at all afraid of them. If he alone were subject to them he would fear them.

ON 'BIRAHA' OR YEARNING FOR THE LORD

[196]

बिना प्रेम धीरज नहीं, बिरह बिना बैराग ।
सदगुरु बिना न छुटिहै, मन मनसा की दाग ॥

Without love there is no patience
  Sans non-attachment separation pain
Without preceptor's grace none can erase
  All his mind's stain.

Kabīr implies that without true love for the Lord there cannot be patience and without non-attachment to worldly connections, the pain of separation from the Lord. He affirms that without the preceptor's grace the stains of life cannot go.

[197]

नैना नीभर लाइया, रहट बसै निस जाम ।
पपिहा ज्यूं 'पिय' 'पिय' करें, कब मिलहुँगे राम ॥

I shall lodge Him in my eye
    And chant His Name always
Papīhā-like 'Piyā', 'Piyā' I will cry
    How soon can I see Rāma, O sage?

Kabīr expresses his deep yearning for the Lord saying that he
would put the Lord in his eye and cry for him like the papīhā
bird calling 'Piyā', 'Piyā' for her love all the time, and wonders
when he will see Him.

[198]

नयना अंतरि आव तूं , ज्यों हौं नैन झंपेउं ।
ना हम देखौं औरको, ना तुभ देखन देउं ॥

Come inside my eye for once
    And I will close my eye
You will see me and none else there
    And You alone I will see.

Kabīr implores the Lord to come inside his eye for once so that
he would drop his eyelid making it impossible for the Lord to
see anybody except him, and for him to see anybody except the
Lord. He expresses his deep and earnest yearning for the Lord.

[199]

सोइ आंसू साजना, सोइ लोग बिगाहिं ।
जो लोहन लोही बुबै, तौ जानौ हेत हियाहिं ॥

The same tear is shed by
    The saint and the sinner
If blood he sheds when he does cry
    Wisdom has dawned in him be sure.

Both the saint and the sinner cry for the mercy of the Lord, the saint for salvation, the sinner for protection. But only if the yearning is intense it can move the Lord. Kabīr figuratively expresses such yearning as shedding tears of blood.

[200]

श्राग जो लगी समंद में, धुंवा न परघट होय ।
सो जाने जो जरमुंञ्रा, जाकी लागी होय ॥

When fire rages in bowel of ocean
    No smoke is formed at all
Only ocean knows being touched by it
    And know the forces that enkindle.

Kabīr points out that when fire rages in the bowel of the ocean due to internal movements of currents and water pressure, no smoke is generated. The intense heat of the fire which is called *vadabā* is felt by the ocean water and the forces which cause it.

Likewise there rages intense turmoil of agony in the heart of the true devotee but the world remains unaware of it. Only the sufferer knows or does the Lord for whose sake the devotee suffers.

[201]

श्राइ न सकौं तुभ पै, सकूं न तुभ बुलाइ ।
जियरा यों ही लेहुँगे, बिरह तपाइ तपाइ ॥

I am unable to come to You
    Or from core of heart invoke
The pang of separation pains me so
    My heart does burn and choke.

The devotee feels helpless as he cannot have a vision of the Lord or even invoke Him properly. The pain of separation from the Lord and the yearning for reunion is so great that it is burning and choking his heart. According to Kabīr the devotee who does not experience this pain cannot get the Lord. (Vide verse No. 203)

[202]

बिरह कहे कबीर सूं , तू जनि छाड़ै मोहि ।
पर ब्रह्म के तेज मैं, तँह ले राखौं तोहि ।

Biraha calls out to Kabīr, "Listen,
    Do not leave me alone
I will take you where the Lord does glisten
    And leave you on your own!"

Biraha or yearning for the Lord asks Kabīr not to leave her
company for she will help him to reach God. Kabīr indicates
that it is intense yearning for the Lord alone that will help one
to realise Him.

[203]

कमोदनी जलहरि बसै, चंदा बसै अकास ।
जो जाही को भावता, सो ताही के पास ॥

The lotus blooms in tanks and lakes
    The moon shines high in sky
Though far apart if one pines for the other
    For him the other is nigh.

The lotus blooms on the earth whereas the moon shines high up
in the sky, but because the lotus pines for the moon, for her the
moon is near at hand though really far away, and like that any
one who pines for another will find that he or she is quite near
though really far away. Kabīr implies that this also applies in the
case of the Lord.

[204]

जाइ पूछो उस घायलै, दिवस पीड़ निस जाग ।
बाहरा हारा जारिग है, कै जारगै जिस लाग ॥

Ask him who has suffered the pain
    Of sleepless nights and days of woes

He knows who has himself suffered
And He for whom the suffering knows.

Kabīr implies that the one who has suffered the pain of pining
for the Lord knows the painful days and wakeful nights undergone by him and also He for whom he suffers knows them, i.e.
the Lord.

ON 'KĀMA' OR LUST, SEX, WOMEN

[205]

काम कहर असवार है, सब को मारे ढाय ।
कोइ एक हरिजन उबरे, जाका राम सहाय ॥

Lust it is that assails all
Gives all its push and pull
Scarce the man who does escape
If by God's grace he is cool.

It is only by God's grace that the self-possessed man can hope to
escape the powerful impact of lust. Kabīr warns that man
should make every effort to resist its push and pull.

[206]

जो कबहूँ के देखिये, बीर बहन कै माय ।
आठ पहर अलग रहै, ताको काल न खाय ॥

If by chance one sees a woman
Should take her as sister or mother
Remain as far he can from her
Death cannot devour.

Kabīr holds lust to be the worst enemy of man. He should avoid
casting his eyes on any woman. If by chance he does see any he
should look upon her as mother or sister. Then death, says
Kabīr, will not assail man. He will become deathless.

[207]

जहां काम तँह नाम नहिं, जहां नाम नहिं काम ।
दोनों कबहूं ना मिलैं, रबि रजनी इक धाम ॥

Lust cannot live near devotion
    Nor devotion near lust's sight
These two can never coexist
    The sun and gloom of night.

Lust and devotion for the Lord cannot coexist like the sun and darkness of the night. Kabīr implies that to subdue lust devotion to the Lord is the best weapon.

[208]

पतिबरता पति को भजै, और ग्रान न सुहाइ ।
सिंह बचा बिजा लंघना, तो भी घास न खाइ ॥

The chaste wife her husband seeks
    None else does she ponder
Does lion cub ever eat grass
    Even if assailed by hunger?

As the cub of a lion will not eat grass even when assailed by hunger so will not the chaste woman crave for any person other than her husband. Kabīr always praises chastity and loyalty of the wife. He implies that like the chaste wife the devotee should also be loyal and devoted to the Lord in order to get His grace.

ON 'SATSAṄGA' OR ASSOCIATION WITH THE NOBLE AND RIGHTEOUS

[209]

तेल तिली सों उपजैं, सदा तेल को तेल ।
संगति को बेरौ भयो, ताते नाम फुलेल ॥

Oil extracted from the oil seed
    Stays oil till the end
It soon becomes sweet scented oil
    As soon essence you blend.

As scent will turn oil fragrant so will holy company turn a sinful worldling into a pure, stainless soul.

[210]

कबीर खाइ कि पानी न पीबे कोय ।
जाय मिले जब गंग में, गंगोदक होय ॥

Says Kabīr, none does ever drink
    The road-side drain-water
But when it mingles in the Ganges
    It becomes *Gaṅgodaka* pure!

The company of the righteous and noble persons has tremendous influence. Kabīr says that the road side drain water after mingling in river Ganges becomes pure *Gaṅgodaka* or sacred and pure Ganges water.

[211]

कबिरा मन पंछी भया, भावै तहँवा जाय ।
जो जैसी संगति करें, तैसा फल खाय ॥

Says Kabīr
The mind-bird flies here and there
    As it suits its mood
So man keeps company of his choice
    Gets result as it is bad or good!

Kabīr implies that man should not be at the beck and call of mind which is restless by nature. He should also not keep company with persons that cannot discriminate between good and evil.

[212]

पसुअों से पाला पड़चो, रह रह हिया न खीज ।
उसर बीज न उगसी, घाल दूना बीज ॥

If with animals you live like them
    You imbibe their baser trait
If the land is infertile
    Can twice the seed germinate?

If man lives with animals following their way of life, traits of
animal nature may surface in him. That will be the effect of keeping bad company. But if one tries to superimpose human nature
on animal nature the former will become inoperative. It will be
like good seed not germinating on infertile soil. Kabir implies
that the baser nature may influence the higher nature, but that it
will be comparatively difficult for the higher nature to influence
the baser nature. It will be like *throwing* away good seeds in an
infertile soil.

ON 'PAROPKĀRA' OR ASSISTANCE AND CHARITY TO OTHERS

[213]

हम देखत जग जात है, जग देखत हम जाहि ।
ऐसा कोइ ना मिला, पकड़ि छुड़ावै बाहि ॥

World is melting before my eyes
    I too shall dissolve
I have not so far seen the man
    Who can pull me from above.

Kabir asserts that all creatures on earth are mortal and all things
are perishable and that the process of dissolution is going on all
the time. It is rare to find one who can pull out another to save
him from perishing. He also affirms that all here are steeped in
selfishness.

[214]

ऐसा कोइ ना मिला, हमको दे उपदेस ।
भौ सागर में डूबते, कर गहि काढ़ें केस ॥

I have not yet seen the man who gives
    All the good advice
And saves others from drowning
    In the worldly sea of vice.

Rare is the man who gives good advice to others and saves them
from the vices of earth. Kabīr implies that men are self-centred
and that such an attitude is neither helpful to themselves nor to
the community. It should be eschewed.

[215]

बाढ़ी आवत देखिकैं, तरवर डोलन लाग ।
हम काटे की कछु नहीं, पंखेरु घर भाग ॥

Seeing the wood-cutter come at it
    The tree does start up and say
"He will fell me—let him do
    But what of the birds that stay?"

One should be more conscious and concerned, implies Kabīr,
about the well-being of others than be self-centred. The tree does
not mind being cut and felled but worries as to what will happen
to the birds that have taken shelter in it.

[216]

फागुन आवत देख करि, बन रुना मन मांहि ।
ऊंची डारी पात है, दिन दिन पीले आंहि ॥

At onset of '*Phālguna*' and spring
    The jungle to itself broods
Now greying is sure at hand
    For leaves of tall tree hoods.

On the advent of the spring season the greying and falling of
leaves starts with the taller trees in the forest. Kabīr implies that
it is the senior and abler members of society who should take on
themselves the onslaught of the common danger to the society,
as the larger trees in the forest behave.

[217]

चिड़ी चोंच भर लै गई, नदी घट्या ना नीर ।
दान दिये धन ना घटै, कह गए दास कबीर ॥

The little bird takes beakful grain
    River its water does not withhold
By giving your wealth does not drain
    So has Kabīr told.

Kabīr says that making gifts does not diminish one's wealth as
taking of beakful of grain by a little bird does not diminish the
grain heap, or the river water does not diminish by extensive use
of it by a large number of people.

[218]

कंचन भो पारस परसि, बहुरि न लोहा होइ ।
चंदन बास पलास बिधि, तुक कहै नाहिं कोइ ॥

Iron made gold by the touchstone
    Is not called iron again
Palāsa near sandal tree made sandal
    Is not called 'Palāsa' by men.

Iron turned gold by the action of touchstone never becomes
iron again and, similarly, the *palāsa* tree turned to sandal by
being near the sandal tree does not become the *palāsa* again.
Kabīr indicates the far reaching effect of the company of the
noble and righteous.

ON 'UPADEŚA' OR ADVICE

[219]

कायें चिणावें मालिया, लांबी भीति उसारि ।
घर तो साढ़ी तीन हाथ, घरणें तो पौरणा चारि ॥

Why O rich! are you building
    A big and lofty home?
Just three and half cubits you need
    More will be burdensome.

Acquisition of wealth in excess of need is detrimental to spiritual
aspirations. Kabīr implies that man should not hanker after
wealth in excess of the minimum need. The ultimate need
of land for a man is barely $3\frac{1}{2}$ cubits. So, craving for even $3\frac{3}{4}$
cubits should be considered more than enough and eschewed.
Multiplying one's wants deviates man from his real purpose.

[220]

सुख के माथे सिल परे, नाम हरी का जाय ।
बलिहारी वा दुख की, पल पल नाम रटाय ॥

Let stone fall on the head of joy
    That drives His Name away
Thanks to woe that makes man take
    The Lord's name night and day.

Kabīr implies that man is apt to forget the Lord in his happiness
and remember Him only in his sorrow. He wants, therefore, to
drive away happiness and live with sorrow. Man should
remember God both in happiness and sorrow.

[221]

मैं मेरी तू जनि करौ, मेरी मूल बिनासी ।
मेरी पग का पैंगड़ा, मेरी गर की फांसी ॥

        Plunge not in 'I' and 'Mine'
            They cause all the wreck
        I and mine are chain for feet
            And noose for the neck.

Man should not get immersed in the thought of 'I' and 'Mine',
for that causes miseries and turns out to be like the chain for
his feet and noose for his neck. Kabir implies that selfishness
ultimately causes fall of man bringing him worries, sorrows and
miseries only and so it should be shunned.

[222]

ना कछु किया ना कर सका, ना कछु करने जोग ।
मैं मेरी जो ठानि कै, दूजी आरपैं लोग ॥

        I could achieve not a thing
            Got no chance whatever
        All are plunged in 'I' and 'Mine'
            On one plea or the other.

Men being steeped in selfishness, each for himself alone, none is
able to achieve his goal nor help others to do so. Kabir indicates
that the evil effects of selfishness harm not only the individual
but the society and so they should be eschewed.

[223]

सीप समुंदर मैं बसे, रटत पियास पियास ।
सकल समंद तिन खागिनै, स्वाती बूंद की आस ॥

        Shell though living in heart of ocean
            Does not drink ocean water
        Wails 'thirst' 'thirst' for *Svāti* rain
            Being assailed by thirst dire.

The shell, though living in the ocean, does not drink its water.
She waits in dire thirst for the rain to fall when the *Svāti* star is

shining in the sky. Kabīr cites the steadfast determination of the shell and implies that man should be as determined as the shell in his efforts to attain his goal. And as the rain water turns into a gem in the shell so shall his anguish turn into bliss when the Lord manifests in him.

[224]

बंधे को बंधा मिला, छुटे कौन उपाय ।
कर सेवा निरबंध की, पल में लेत छुड़ाय ।।

One himself bonded gets bonded guide
    How can he get the clue?
Let him seek who has earned salvation
    In moments he can free him too.

One who is himself bonded and has not attained salvation cannot guide another to attain it. Only he who has himself attained the goals of self-realisation can help others to attain it in no time. Kabīr also implies that in selecting the guide or preceptor one has to be careful to choose the right type of master.

[225]

कथनी थोथी जगत में, करनी उत्तम सार ।
कहत कबीर करनी सफल, उतरे मंजिल पार ।।

Idle talks are useless vain
    Good deeds are best of all
Says Kabīr, they lead man to success
    And help him reach his goal.

Idle gossip which is useless should be shunned and man should engage in good deeds which will lead him to success in reaching the goal viz. God.

[226]

सब ग्राहै इस एक मैं, डाल पात फल फूल ।
कबिरा पीछे क्यों रहा, गहि पकड़ा जब मूल ।।

Says Kabīr,
In the tree all these are there
    The flower, the leaf, the fruit
Why should any lag behind
    If he has caught hold of the root?

In the tree are all its various parts viz. the flower, the leaf, and fruit, etc. but one who has caught hold of its root, has all these at his command. Kabīr implies that he who has realised the Lord, the cause and the essence of the world, has got all that the world in its entirety has in it. Nothing remains beyond his reach.

[227]

नींद निसानी मोथ की, उठ कबीर जाग ।
और रसायन छाड़िकै, सांइ रसायन लाग ॥

Says Kabīr,
Sleep is same as death
    Shun indolence awake
Leave aside the other ones
    Lord's Nectar do partake.

According to Kabīr sleep is same as death and so man should shake off indolence and, turning his attention away from distractions, he should concentrate on chanting the Name of the Lord, which is the best alchemy for inducting higher realisation.

[228]

कबीर तहां न जाइये, स्त्री पूछे क्या काम ।
स्वामी कहे न बैठना, फिर फिर पूछे नाम ॥

Says Kabīr, do not go there
    Where housewife asks 'Why came'?
Her husband does not offer a seat
    Asks again and again your name.

Citing a very commonplace example Kabīr advises not to go to
that place where the housewife by way of welcome asks what is
the work that has brought him there and the husband instead of
offering a seat asks his name again and again. This will enable
one to avoid loss of peace of mind that stands in the way of his
spiritual effort, implies Kabīr.

[229]

सबद बराबर धन नहीं, जो कोइ जाणै बोल ।
हीरा तो दामै मिलै, सबद ही मोल न तोल ॥

Speech is the most precious wealth
    If one knows what to speak
Diamond one can buy with money
    Speech is priceless gem to seek.

Kabīr considers speech as the most valuable wealth of man.
Diamond which is considered as most precious can be bought
with money. Speech is even more valuable than that, it is
invaluable.

[230]

गांठी होय सो हाथ कर, हाथ होय सो देय ।
आगे हाट न बाणिया, लेना है तो लेय ॥

Amassed wealth should be taken in hand
    And given away in charity
There is no market ahead for spending it
    On purpose better than bounty.

Amassed wealth is best spent on charity to the poor and needy.
There is no use hoarding wealth with the hope of spending it
later. After death one will have no chance to lay his hands on it.

[231]

सम्पै देखि न हरषियै, बिपति देखि न रोय ।
ज्यों सम्पै त्यों बिपति है, बिधि ने रच्या सो होय ॥

Do not laugh in your weal
Do not cry in woe
Both of them are caused by God
According to His plan you know.

Both prosperity and adversity are caused by God according to His plan. So man should take them in his stride without glee or grief. Kabīr implies that prosperity in the shape of material wealth may be the cause of adversity like personal danger from robbers and induce man to forget the Lord as well. (Vide verse nos. 237 and 220)

[232]

कबिरा घास न निंदिये, जो पांवों तलि होय ।
उड़ि पड़े जब आंख में, खारा बुहेला होय ॥

Says Kabīr, do not decry the grass
That is under your feet
Beware if it floats up to eye
It may harm your sight.

The grass that remains under the feet should not be belittled for if it accidentally flies up and falls in one's eye it may cause harm to the eye. Kabīr implies that the humble and small man should not be disparaged because of his humble and low position; he should be given due respect, and honour as any other man. In another of his couplets, Kabīr cautions not to oppress the weak as his sigh of sorrow is capable of causing ample harm to the oppressor (Elsewhere).

[233]

तीर तुपक से जो लड़ें, सो तो सूर न होइ ।
माया तजि भकति करें, सूर कहावें सोइ ॥

He is not a hero who does fight
With mere bow and arrow

But who kills attachment and is devout
 He is the real hero.

According to Kabīr, the real hero is one who kills his attachment
to bonds of earth and is devoted to the Lord and not he who
fights with bow and arrow.

[234]

तन पबित्र सेवा किये, धन पबित्र किये दान ।
मन पबित्र हरि भजन से, इस बिधि हो कल्यान ॥

Service to others makes body pure
 Wealth is made pure when given to poor
To purify mind meditate the Sire
 You shall get His blessing be sure.

According to Kabīr, the body is purified by rendering service to
others, wealth by giving to the poor and needy, mind by
meditating on the Lord. That is the way to earn God's blessing.

[235]

चिंटी चावल ले चली, बीच में मिल गयी दार ।
कह कबीर दोउ ना मिलें, एक् लें दूजी डार ॥

Says Kabīr,
The little ant carrying rice in mouth
 Finds grain of pulse on way
One of the two he must discard
 Both he cannot convey.

Kabīr advises that man must forsake greed and should be
prepared to discard even a boon he comes by if it is in excess of
his ability to possess or to utilise. The ant has to choose between
the bit of pulse and the grain of rice. It cannot carry both.

[236]

पानी बाढ़ें नाव में, घर में बाढ़ें दाम ।
दोनों हाथ उलचिये, यही सज्जन को काम ॥

If water spills into the boat
    And wealth is amassed at home
With both your hands do throw them out
    Wise men do the same.

Citing the conduct of wise men Kabir advises that when water
spills into the boat, and money is amassed at home they should
be thrown out with both hands in the interest of personal safety.
He also implies that wealth hinders spiritual progress.

[237]

गोधन गजधन बाजिधन, और रतन धन खान ।
जो आवै सन्तोष धन, सब धन धूरि समान ॥

Cattle, wealth and gold and silver
    All such wealth you mind
Are just like dust before contentment
    That is the best wealth you will find!

Kabir affirms that contentment is the best of all kinds of wealth
that a man can possess. He implies that a contented mind gains
poise which is essential for spiritual progress, and that material
wealth and prosperity cannot make a man happy and contented.
On the other hand they make man forget the Lord. This is a
matter of common observation.

[238]

कबिरा भंबर में बैठकै. भौचक मना न जोय ।
डूबन के भय छांड़िये, करता करै सो होय ॥

Says Kabir,
In the midst of perilous whirl
        Lose not courage and common sense

Give up all the fear of drowning
It is God alone who dispenses.

Man should not lose courage and patience when overtaken by
calamity. It is only God who dispenses and so no one need be
worried. One should rather pray to Him for succour.

[239]

ग्यानी से कहिये कहा, कहत कबीर लजाय ।
अंधे आगे नाचते, कला अकारथ जाय ॥

Says Kabir,
I am ashamed to tell the wise
As well informed is his mind
And if I tell the nescient
It will be like dance for the blind.

Kabir says that there is no use telling the wise for he already
knows all that one wants to convey. On the other hand, telling
the unknowing people will be equally useless like showing the
delicate art of dance to the sightless. Kabir implies that there is
no use carrying coal to New Castle nor to sow seeds on infertile
soil.

[240]

खुस खाना है खीचरी, जाहि परा टुक नोंन ।
मांस पराया खाय करी, गरा कटावे कौन ॥

Slightly salted *khicadi*
Is quite tasty fare
Why then should one lose his head
Craving flesh of another?

A simple fare of rice and pulse with sprinkling of a little salt is
ideal food for any, says Kabir. Why should then he crave
animal's meat and be hauled up for killing of the animal?

[241]

प्रेम प्रीत से जो मिलै, ता सो मिलिये धाय ।
श्रंतर राखै जो मिलै, ता सों मिलै बलाय ॥

Who with love befriends you
Accept him with open arms
Who comes to you with crookedness
Keep him at arm's distance.

If one meets you with an open mind and affection he should be welcomed, but he who does so with reservation and a crooked mind should be kept at a distance.

[242]

समभा समभा एक है, श्रनसमभा सब एक ।
समभा सोइ जानिये, जाके हृदय बिबेक ॥

All the wise men feel alike
The fools too in own way
He is really wise in whom
Conscience has the say.

Kabir asserts that all the wise men feel and react in one way and so do the fools in their own way. According to him the real wise man is one who listens to the words of his conscience.

[243]

रूखा सूखा खायके, ठण्डा पाणी पीब ।
देखि परायी चोपड़ी, मत ललचावै जीब ॥

Do not at all tempted be
By the rich man's richer food
In truth, your dry and coarse fare
And pure water that is good!

Kabir commends simple food which is better than the rich man's food full of fat and sweets. One should never crave for that, out of greed.

[244]

प्रभुता को सब कोइ भजै, प्रभु को भजै न कोइ ।
कह कबीर प्रभु को भजै, प्रभुता चेरी होइ ॥

Says Kabīr,
Everyone is running after power
        None pays heed to its Source
He who heeds the Source, the Lord,
        Power will make him its boss.

The Lord is the source of all power and prosperity, but man runs
after power forgetting Him. If he paid heed to Him, power and
prosperity would run after him, asserts Kabīr.

[245]

सिर राखे सिर जात है, सिर काटे सिर सोय ।
जैसे बाती दीप की, काटि उजियारा होय ॥

You lose your head by keeping it
        Sacrifice makes it greater
Like the wick of the burning lamp
        Flick its head it shines better.

Citing the example of the burning lamp which burns brighter if
the wick-head is flicked from time to time. Kabīr asserts that if
one sacrifices his head, or, in other words, surrenders himself
completely to the Lord, he attains salvation or the highest boon
from God. He also implies that man will fall off his purpose if
he does not surrender himself to the Lord as the lamp will shine
dim if its wick-head is not flicked.

ON 'DARŚANA' OR PHILOSOPHICAL
AND SPIRITUAL TOPICS

[246]

हिन्दु कहे राम मोहि प्यारा, तुरक कहै रहिमाना ।
आपस में दोउ लरि लरि मुए, मरम न काहू जाना ॥

Hindu says Rāma is dear to him
  Muslim says Rahīm
Both quarrel, fight and kill each other
  Not knowing the root of thing.

The Hindu proclaims that Rāma is the God dear to him while the Turak (Muslim) declares Rahīm as his God, but not knowing that fundamentally both are one and the same, they quarrel over this, fight each other and court death. God of the universe is only one and the different names given to Him in different faiths cannot create more than one God. Both Hindus and Turaks should realise this and refrain from hostilities over inessential matters, implies Kabīr.

[247]

मूल कबीरा गहि चढ़ें, फल खाय भरि पेट ।
चौरासी का भय नहीं, ज्यों चाहै त्यों लेट ॥

With help of root Kabīr rides the tree
  Eats ripe fruits to fill
Of birth-death-cycle is carefree
  Sleeps and snores at will!

Kabīr affirms that whosoever understands the import and takes help of the root or essence of things does not have to face miseries. On the other hand, he gains happiness and also freedom from the cycle of rebirths. By root Kabīr implies the Lord and indicates that if a man takes God for his shelter he succeeds in his spiritual endeavour to attain salvation.

[248]

ऐसा कोइ ना मिला, सब बिधि देय बताय ।
सुन्न महल में पुरुस है, ताहि रहूं लौ लाय ॥

I have not so far seen the one
  To teach me all the ways

Of deeply loving the Formless God
In the unseen void space!

Rare is the man who can instruct one on the ways of realising
and deeply loving the Formless God in the unseen void. Kabīr
has not come across even one.

[249]

घटका परदा खोलकैं, सनमुख लै दीदार ।
बाल सनेही सांइया, आदि व्रत का यार ॥

Remove the screen that engulfs you
And meet Him face to face
Your only Friend from your birth
Till end of your days.

The screen of *Māyā* or illusion enfolds man on earth. If one is
able to remove this screen he will be able to see the Lord face to
face. Kabīr asserts that He is the only Friend from the beginning till the end of life.

[250]

हद बेहद दोउ तजी, अबरन किया मिलान ।
कहे कबीर ता दास पर, बारौं सरल जहान ॥

Says Kabīr, beyond the finite, and the infinite
Whoever has met the Formless God
I shall be his slave, and shower on him
All splendours of the world.

The Formless God is beyond the finite and the infinite. Kabīr
implies that God is inscrutable and that he will be a slave to
him whoever has realised Him and shower all the splendours of
the earth on his feet.

[251]

हिंदू तुरक के बीच मै, सब्द कहूं निरबान ।
बंधन काटूं जगत का, मैं रहता रहिमान ॥

Says Kabīr,
I bring the message of salvation
    To the Hindu and Musalmān
And of snapping the bonds of earth
    But I am with no one.

Kabīr says that he brings the message of salvation to both
Hindus and Muslims, and of snapping the bonds of earth, but
he himself remains above both Hindus and Muslims. Kabīr
implies that though he seeks their emancipation, he does not
identify himself with either of the faiths.

[252]

तत्त तलैं की सो कहै, तत्त तलैं का होय ।
माझ महल की को कहै, पड़दा गाढ़ा सोय ॥

He can say who does possess
    Insight of ultimate knowledge
None can say even of the things of earth
    For we remain here in slumber and haze.

It is only he who has insight of the ultimate knowledge of things
that can speak about it, but such men are rare and most of the
men are either in sleep or in ignorance and perplexity. We cannot rightly speak even of the earthly things being always in
sleep and mental confusion, deplores Kabīr.

[253]

कतेक सिब संकर गए उठि, राम समाधि अबहुं नहिं छुटी ॥
प्रलय काल कहुं कतेक भास, गए इंद्र सो अगणित लास ॥
ब्रह्मा खोजि पर्यो गहि नाल, कहे कबीर ये राम निराल ॥

Gone are countless Śiva and Śaṅkara
    Yet Rāma is in deep meditation
Since the Deluge Ages are over
    Countless Indras have come and gone
Says Kabīr, Brahmā still seeks the Essence
    Of Lord Rāma's mystic presence.

The Supreme God, Lord Rāma, is in eternal meditation and in the meantime countless Indras (the rain God) have come and gone. It is Ages since the great Deluge took place Brahmā (the God in charge of creation) is still seeking the essence of Lord Rāma but has not succeeded in getting it. Kabīr indicates a brief outline of the status of the Supreme Deity Rāma.

[254]

हँस हँस कंत न पाइये, जिन पाया तिनि रोय ।
जो हँसी ही हरि मिलैं, तो नाहिं दुहागिनि होय ॥

One cannot smile and get the Lord
    Only those who weep can get
If to smile He did respond
    None would be Lord-bereft.

No one has got the Lord in response to light heartedness. If that were so no one would be without the Lord. On the other hand, only he who has pined and wept for the Lord has realised Him. Kabīr implies that God-realisation is gained the hard way.

[255]

दुरलभ मानिस जनम है, होय न दूजी बार ।
पक्का फल जो गिर पड़्या, लगे न दूजी बार ॥

Human life is precious rare
    We do not get it again
Like ripe fruit that drops from tree
    Can it ever rejoin?

Human life is a rare gift of God. It is not secured for a second time, the end of one's life being the end of it once for all. It is like a ripe fruit which falls off a tree, never to rejoin it. Human life should, therefore, be utilised properly to attain salvation by pursuing righteous living and surrendering to the Lord. If one fails in this he slides down for rebirth in a lower gene again and again till he gets rebirth as a human being and chance to strive for his salvation.

[256]

कांचे भांडे से रहे ज्यूं कुम्हार का नेह ।
भीतर से रक्षा करे, बाहर चोट देह ॥

The potter cares for the fresh clay pot
    Protects from inside with his palm
And strikes from above to shape it up
    Cures the defects by this balm.

The potter carefully shapes the raw earthen pot by putting his protective palm from inside and beating it up from above to give it a proper shape. The Lord likewise takes care of His devotee by putting him to trials and tribulations and protecting him all the time from falling thereby giving him the opportunity to gather experience and skill in the art of righteous living.

[257]

गुर नहीं, चेला नहीं, मुरीद हूँ नहिं पीर ।
एक नहीं दूजा नहीं, बिलमै दास कबीर ॥

Neither *Guru* nor *Celā* I am
    Neither Murīd nor Pīr
I am neither the one nor the other
    Sitting tight I am Kabīr.

Kabīr implies that he does not belong to any particular faith. He asserts that he is what he is. Kabīr attached the greatest importance to one's own realisation of the Lord rather than to one's adherance to any particular faith, or creed.

[258]

कितने मनाऊँ पांव परि, कितने मनाऊं रोय ।
हिंदू पूजैं देबता, तुरक न काहू कोय ॥

How many shall I pray to tell
And weep to tell how many
Yet Hindus worship God in temple
And Muslims do not any.

In Kabīr's view it is neither rewarding to offer worship to the
stone idols in the temple (instead of the God within) as do the
Hindus nor to take shelter of no God for attaining salvation (as
do the Muslims). He holds that God who dwells in the heart of
every being is the one whose shelter has to be sought by complete
self-surrender to Him.

[259]

लंबा मारग दूर घर, बिकट पंथ बहु मार ।
कहो संतो क्यों पाइये, दुर्लभ हरि दीदार ॥

Far is your home, O saint!
And perilous is the road
Tell me how you travel it
And meet your rare Lord?

The path of devotion for the realisation of the Lord is difficult
and long, beset with many hazards. Kabīr implies that the devotee has to be up and doing and cautious in his efforts to reach
the goal and meet the Lord.

[260]

कबीर निर्भय राम भज, जब लगि दीवै बाती ।
तेल घट्या बाती बुझी, तब सोबै दिन राती ॥

Says Kabīr,
As long the lamp is burning
Recite God's Name sans fright

Soon as oil will finish and lamp go out
Man shall sleep all day and night.

Kabīr implies that man may be overtaken by death anytime
without warning. So he should chant the Lord's name all the
time instead of indulging in sleep. When death comes he will
sleep for ever; let him, therefore, remain awake and meditate on
the Lord's name each and every moment vouchsafed to him.

[261]

दीपक ग्यान सबद धुनि घंटा । परम पुरुस तँह देब अनंता ।
परम प्रकास सकर उजियारा । कहै कबीर मैं दास तुम्हारा ॥

Before the Lord I shall offer
Candles of knowledge, bells of prayer
Where shines the Lord in eternal glow
His slave, Kabīr, stands there.

Mental supplication to the Formless God in the form of prayer
and self-surrender is far more rewarding than *pūjā*, offering of
flowers and candles in the temple.

[262]

कबीर सो धन संचिये, जो आगे कूं होय ।
सीस चढ़ाये पोटली, ले जात देख्या न कोय ॥

Says Kabīr,
Save only that wealth
That later may be useful
And if you carry it on head in a bundle
To others will not be visible.

Spiritual wealth, being invisible to the eye, is not subject to theft
or burglary. Kabīr indicates that man should collect and save
that wealth and not the worldly riches. The former will bring
him emancipation while the latter only worries and miseries.

[263]

कबीर हरि के नाम सूं, प्रीति रहे इकतार ।
तौ मुख ते मोती भरे, हीरा श्रंत न पार ॥

Says Kabīr,
Whoever bears in his heart
    Love for the Lord's Name
Pearls from his lips do flow
    His heart is aglow with diamond flame.

Kabīr implies that whosoever has in his heart love for the Lord's Name, his words of mouth become noble and sweet and his heart illumined and enlightened.

[264]

जहाँ जुरा मरण व्याधी नहीं, मुआ न सुणिये कोइ ।
चला कबिरा तिहि देस ड़े, जहाँ बंद बिधाता होइ ॥

Where old age and disease assail not
    And death is not heard of
There Kabīr is set ready to go
    Where Guardian Angel is God Himself.

Kabīr is yearning for the land of the Lord where there is no old age and disease to assail him and where God Himself is the Guardian Angel, i.e. sole refuge. He implies that man should crave for that blissful land by surrendering to the Lord in order to be free from the sufferings of the world.

[265]

गगन गरजै तहां सदा पावस भरे
होत झनकार नित बाजत तूरा ।
बेद कतेब की गति नाहीं तहां
कहै कबीर कोइ रमें सूरा ॥

Says Kabīr,
The sky rumbles there
        With eternal music, Nectar rains
    Where Veda and Kurān have no passage
        Only true hero his access gains.

According to Kabīr, the Formless God dwells in the void of the sky where eternal music swells and Nectar rains all the time. Scriptures like Veda or Kurān have no place there. Only the true hero has access to it. In Kabīr's view the real hero is one who has taken all the pains to traverse the long and arduous way and severed and laid his head at the Lord's feet, i.e. who has completely surrendered himself to the Lord. He alone can reach there, affirms Kabīr. Reference to thunder and lightening and music is fairly common in Kabīr's writing. It is taken for the state of the manifestation of the *nāda*, the mysterial sound that stills the mind into self-realisation.

[266]

कबीर सबद सरीर में, बिन गुन बाजे तांति ।
बाहर भीतर रमि रह्या, ताते छूटी भरांति ।

Says Kabīr,
The stringless *veeṇā* within
        The Lord's Name ever sings
    The music does pervade out and in
        And dispels doubts and falterings.

The stringless instrument in the body chants the Lord's Name ceaselessly and that pervades the entire body with the result that doubts of the mind and wavering are dispelled, says Kabīr. He implies that the breathing process is an endless recital of the Lord's Name, and if one pays proper heed to it he will be transformed thereby. Kabīr is also referring to the redemptive sound of the *nāda* which a Yogī experiences within him.

[267]

कबीर मारग कठिन है, कोइ न सकइ जाइ ।
गए तो बहुरे नाहिं, कुसल कहे को आइ ॥

Difficult is the path says Kabīr
　　None can reach the goal
The few who do, they never return,
　　Who can portray at all?

Long and arduous is the path to the land of the Lord. Few are
able to tread it and reach their goal. But these blessed souls do
not return from their blissful state to our dark, unhappy world.
So none is there to tell us what is that state they call the state
of god-realisation. Kabīr implies that only on attaining salvation
does a man reach there and such a soul has no rebirth.

[268]

कहे कबीरा दास फकीरा, अपनी राह चलि भाइ ।
हिन्दु तुरक का करता एकै, ता गति लह्या न जाइ ॥

Says Kabīr,
One and same is the Supreme Lord
　　Of Hindu and Muslim
But they both do not realise Him
　　In their own way remain groping.

Kabīr affirms repeatedly that the Lord is one and the same for
people of all religious faiths and communities. There cannot be
two or more Gods for the Universe, one for each faith. That
would lead to the ruin of the universe.

[269]

हिन्दु तुरक दोउ रहे टूटी फूटी अरु कनराइ ।
अरध उरध दस दिस जित तित पूरि रह्या रामराइ ॥

> Both Hindu and Turak are mistaken
> They do not have the notion
> The Great Lord Rāma does permeate
> The universe in every direction.

Kabīr deplores that the Hindus and Muslims do not realise that the Lord is omnipresent. They try to find Him in different places considered sacred by each of them according to their belief and tradition.

[270]

काबा फिर कासी भया, राम भया रहीम ।
मोट चून मेंदा भया, बैठि कबीरा जीम ॥

Says Kabīr,
> In essence Kābbā is same as Kāśī
> Rāma and Rahīm are same
> Same is the powder of all the grains
> Man eats all of them.

The difference in names does not matter if fundamentally things are the same. It is like the powder of different edible grains which men eat. For Hindus *Kāśī* is the sacred place, and for the Muslims Kābbā. They consider these places holy because they are associated with prophets and men of God. Muslims call God Rahīm and Hindus Call Him Rāma. Only names are different, the essence is the same. Thus does Kabīr highlight the futility of fanaticism and also the affinity of different faiths.

[271]

बसुधा बन बहु भांती, फूल्या फूलौ अगाध ।
मिस्ट सुबास कबीर गहि, बिसम कहै किहि साध ॥

Says Kabīr,
> In the woods of the world
> Fruits and flowers abound

He who learnt to pick and choose
    Sweet fruits and flowers he found;
Others failed to choose and pick
    Thought the world unsound.

For want of the know-how man gropes in the dark and fails
to find and pick sweet flowers and fruits with which the earth
abounds and so he wrongly blames the ways of the world. Kabīr
indicates that human life offers the best chance to earn salvation by following righteous living and by complete surrender
to the Lord. Without the know-how man loses the chance and
takes rebirth till he gets human life again to get the next chance.

ON 'JĪVĀTMĀ', 'PARAMĀTMĀ' AND 'MOKṢA' OR SOUL, SUPREME SOUL AND SALVATION

[272]

बिरछा पूछै बीज सों, बीज बृछ के मार्हि ।
जीव सो ढूंडे ब्रह्म को, ब्रह्म जीव के पार्हि ॥

Says the tree "O, seed, you see
    How within me you are
Like though the Lord is in every being
    Man seeks Him here and there."

The Supreme Soul abides in man as the seed abides in the tree.
Still man would seek the ultimate reality not within himself; he
would seek it outside. Kabīr calls upon man to follow the
internal way if he wants to realise God. Self-realisation alone is
God-realisation, indicates Kabīr.

[273]

जीवत समभैं जीवत बुझैं, जीवत ही करो आस ।
जीवत करम की फांस न काटी, मुये मुक्ति की आस ॥

Alive you can see and know it all
  So in life crave salvation
Bonds of earth you did not snap in life
  On death you crave, what fun!

If one can snap the bonds of earth and earnestly crave for salvation he can attain it and know it all during life time. There is no point in craving for it on death without having snapped the bonds of earth in life, says Kabīr.

[274]

पांछी उड़ा गगन को, धड़ रहा परदेस ।
पानी पीवे चोंच बिन, भूल गया वा देस ॥

The swan flew up the unknown skies
  Free from her gross form
Beakless she drank water there
  Forgetting her earthly home.

'Swan' is the dead man's soul. It is believed that on death the soul leaves the body clothed in a subtle covering provided by the human body. Depending on the condition of this subtle covering, the course of journey of the soul is determined. If, as a result of sustained righteous conduct, it is in fresh and bright condition the soul with the covering goes to heaven through the *devayāna mārga* (heavenly way) to meet and mingle with the Supreme Soul never to be reborn. If, on the other hand, man indulges in evil deeds, the covering becomes pale and dull. In such a case the soul, along with the subtle covering, has to enter a lesser gene here on earth immediately on release from the dead body. It does not go heavenward.

Here Kabīr makes mention of the first category where the soul has the upward journey to heaven.

[275]

एक एक तें ब्रंत हूँ , ब्रंत एक हूँ जाय ।
एक से एक परचे भया, एकै माहिं समाय ॥

One craved union with the Other One
  At last they became One
Each of them recognised the other
  United and mingled into One.

The soul of man (*jīvātmā*) craves union with the Supreme Soul
(*Paramātmā*). They approach and recognise each other and
mingle into one. The soul of man gets dissolved in the Supreme
Soul leaving no trace of itself behind. Kabīr believes in the ulti-
mate identity of the ātman (*jīvātmā*) and Brahman (Supreme
Soul or *Paramātmā*).

[276]

कहै कबीर बिचार करि, वो पद है निरबान ।
सत लै मन में राखिये, जहां न दूजी ग्रान ॥

Be firm of Truth in mind
  Says Kabīr with conviction
And hold nothing else inside
  That is the road to salvation.

Firm adherance to Truth is the surest way to salvation and a
second like that is not there. Kabīr calls upon man to adhere
firmly to truth and truth alone.

[277]

जीबनते मरिबो भलो, जो मरि जाणै कोय ।
मरिबा पहिले जो मरे, तो कलि अचरज होय ॥

Death is better far than life
  If one knows how to die
He who dies before death does come
  In 'Kali', amazing this may be.

By 'dying before death' Kabīr implies attaining salvation or
becoming deathless. Man on earth being egocentric does not
succeed in his spiritual efforts. One who succeeds in killing his

ego will succeed in attaining salvation in life. This may appear to be an amazing feat in the current Kali Yuga or the Age of vices. 'Kali' known as 'Kali Yuga' is the last of the four Yugas or Ages, viz., Satya, Treta, Dvāpara and Kali, according to the Hindu conception.

[278]

उलटि समाना आप में, प्रगटी जोत अनंत ।
साहब सेबक एक संग, खेलें सदा बसंत ॥

On return soul mingles in Supreme Soul
    In Heavenly effulgence
Where Master and servant do mingle
    Eternal spring prevails.

Kabīr implies that the soul of man (*Jīvātmā*) craves union with the Supreme Soul (*Paramātmā*) and when they mingle into One in Heavenly effulgence there is eternal spring and greenery all around. Kabīr figuratively designates the Supreme Soul as Master and the human soul (*Jīvātmā*) as servant.

[279]

घर जाले घर उबरै, घर राखौं घर जाइ ।
एक अचंभा देखिया, मड़ा काल को खाइ ।

If you burn your house you save it
    If preserved it goeth
I have noticed an amazing feat
    Of the dead devouring death.

Kabīr affirms that if one kills his ego and bonds of the earth he attains his salvation or heavenly abode, his primordial home. Death of ego means death of death itself. For death is nothing other than the body-ego. By "if preserved it goeth" Kabīr implies that if ego and attachment to bonds of earth persist, man loses the chance of salvation or getting a foothold in his real home, i.e. heaven.

[280]

जल में कुंभ कुंभ में जल है, बाहर भीतर पानी ।
फूटा कुंभ जल जलहिं समाना, इहि तत् कथ्यो ग्यानी ॥

When in water the pitcher is dipped
In and out there is water
If pitcher breaks the waters mingle
To the wise the import is clear.

When a pitcher is dipped in water there is water both in the
pitcher and without it. If the pitcher breaks then both the
waters mingle without distinction. Kabīr implies that when the
soul of man (Jīvātmā) mingles in the Supreme Soul (Paramātmā)
there is complete union and both become indistinguishably one.

[281]

हेरत हेरत हे सखी, हेरत गया हिराय ।
बूंद समानी समंद में, सो कित हेरत जाय ॥

Seeking and searching all the time
I lost my own track
When drop of water falls in ocean
How can one get it back?

Kabīr refers to the union of the soul of man (Jīvātmā) and the
Supreme Soul (Paramātmā or God). The soul is part of the
Supreme Soul, and on the salvation, it mingles completely in
the latter and the two cannot be distinguished from each other
however much one tries. A search will be futile, Kabīr indicates.

ON 'GARVA' OR PRIDE

[282]

कबिरा गर्ब न कीजिये, ऊंचा देखि आबास ।
काल परौ भुंइ लेटना, ऊपर जमसी घास ॥

Says Kabīr,
One should not be arrogant
　　Seeing his high mansion
On death he will lie on bare land
　　And grass will grow thereon.

One should not be proud of his big mansion, warns Kabīr, for on death he will be laid in the ground which will overgrow with grass in due course.

[283]

सकता सूकर कूकरा, तीनों के गति एक ।
कोटि जतन परमोधिये, तऊ न छाड़ें टेक ॥

The scoundrel, the swine, and the dog
　　Same is their make
Whatever heroic effort one makes
　　Arrogance they cannot forsake.

The swine, the dog and the scoundrel are of the same nature being highly arrogant and they can never abandon arrogance. Kabīr implies that man is endowed with intellect, wisdom, and conscience, and he should be able to eschew pride by his own effort.

[284]

काहे कुं छायें ऊंच ऊंचेरा साढ़े तीन हाथ घर मेरा ।
कहे कबीर नर गरब न कीजें, जेता तन तेता लीजें ॥

Says Kabīr,
Why you raise a mansion
　　Just three and half cubits you need
Listen, pride you must forsake
　　For more you should not bid.

Kabīr harps on the inadvisability of craving for more wealth and worldly possessions like land in excess of one's minimum need. There is no need to build large mansions when ultimately one requires only three and a half cubits of land for his body to be laid after death, he says in a figurative way.

[285]

जग में बैरी कोउ नहीं, जो मन सीतल होय ।
इस आपा को डारि दे, दया कर सब कोय ॥

He who has banished anger
And also pride from mind
To everyone is kind, and dear
Has no enemy to find.

One who is sober and cool by temperament has no enemy on earth. Man should give up his ego and be compassionate to others. Then there will be no enemy of him, Kabīr affirms.

[286]

सिंह अकेला बन रहे, पलक पलक करे दौर ।
जैसे बन अपना, तैसा मन है और ॥

Alone the lion roams in the forest
Thinks it is all his domain
Like that the mind roams on the earth
Thinking it is all its own.

Like the lion roaming in the forest taking it as his personal property, the mind roams over the whole world thinking that it is all its own. Kabīr implies that man should shed his ego by all means.

[287]

या दुनिया में आइके, छाड़ि देय तू ऐंठ ।
लेना है सो लेइ लें, उठी जात है पेंठ ॥

Being born here on earth as man
Give up your arrogance
Buy quickly what you wish to gain
The market may close at once.

Kabīr has laid great stress on discarding pride or ego for attaining success and also on giving up laziness as life is transient.

[288]

गही टेक छाड़े नहीं, जीभ चोंच जरि जाय ।
मीठा कहा श्रंगार में, ताहि चकोर चबाय ॥

Pride is so difficult to shun
Though it wounds one and all
Like 'Cakora' though its beak may burn
Sticks to the insipid burning coal.

Mistaking the burning red coal for a ripe fruit *cakora* puts her beak into it. But out of her ego she is not prepared to own up her mistake and goes on picking up the burning coal. Like that man is caught in the web of his ego and not able to release himself from its clutches. Kabīr implies that he should make every effort to shake off pride.

ON 'BOLĪ' OR WORDS OF MOUTH

[289]

कुटिल बचन सबसे बुरा, जारि तन करे छार ।
साधु बचन जल रूप है, बरसे अमृत धार ॥

Harsh word is worst of all
Burns its target to ash
Sweet word is like Heaven's nectar
It pleases cools, does not harass.

Harsh words, like burning fire, burn to ash their target viz. the person addressed to while sweet words please and cool and do not harass. Kabīr has laid great emphasis on correct and balanced speech.

[290]

सहज तराजू आनि करि, सब रस देखे तोलि ।
सब रस मांहि जीभ रस, जो कोइ जारणे बोलि ॥

I have weighed and watched with care
  Sweetness of all kind
That of the tongue is sweeter far
  If you use it well, you mind.

After carefully weighing the sweetness of all kinds of sweets it is found that the sweetness of the tongue is the best of all sweets. Kabīr has repeatedly emphasised the importance of maintaining the sweetness of the word of the mouth.

[291]

साधु भया तो क्या भया, जो नहिं बोल बिचार ।
हतै पराइ आतमा, जीभ लिये तरबार ॥

What if one is a learned saint
  His tongue is sans control
Wielding the sword of vile words
  He wounds one and all.

If one is not able to control his tongue he will wound others with the sword of wild and vile words. His learning in the scriptures will be of no avail to him. Kabīr also implies that on the other hand the reaction of it will cause loss of peace of mind to himself and thereby be an impediment to his spiritual efforts.

ON 'MOHA' OR BONDS OF EARTH (ATTACHMENT)

[292]

हम घर जारा अपना, लूका लीन्हा हाथ ।
वाहुका घर फूंकहूँ, जो चले हमारे साथ ॥

I have burnt my house down
    With fire brand in hand
I shall burn his house who comes
    And also joins my band.

Kabīr indicates that he has snapped his worldly connections
completely and that he would snap them for any one who wants
to join him. He implies that worldly attachments are an impediment to spiritual pursuits and should be snapped in order to
embark on the spiritual path.

[293]

कबीर माया मोहिनी, मारे जान सुजान ।
भागाही छूटे नहीं, भरि भरि मारे बान ॥

Says Kabīr,
Attachment is like a tempting woman
    Bewitches even the wise man
Does not leave although driven
    Tries to hit again and again.

Attachment causes fall of even a wise man as does a seductive
woman of the lustful. Even when driven away, it comes back
again and again to bewitch and bewilder its target, says Kabīr.
He implies that it is difficult to overcome worldly attachment.

[294]

कबीर मेरा कोइ नहीं, हम काहू के नाहिं ।
परै पहुँचा नाव ज्यौ, मिलिकें बिछुड़ी जाहिं ॥

Says Kabīr,
None is mine in the wide world
    And I belong to none
Unconcerned I go as at Journey's end
    Each traveller goes on his own.

One should live quite unattached to anybody or anything on earth, implies Kabīr. Though living in society he should be able to part company from the others in an unconcerned manner like travellers parting company at end of the journey. Non-attachment will bring peace of mind which is essential for spiritual progress.

MISCELLANEOUS

[295]

डाल जो ढूंड़ै मूल को, डाल मूल के पाहिं ।
श्राप आप को सब चलैं, मिलै मूल सों नाहिं ॥

The branch seeks the root of tree
    Not seeing it at the foot
Each one moves in his own way
    Seeing not the root.

The branch searched for the root but could not notice it at the foot of the tree. Kabīr says that when everyone moves in his own way no one takes notice of the root which is the most vital part and implies that, that is why man gropes in the dark. He also implies that man faces bewilderment on earth because he fails to take refuge in the Lord who is the Creator or root of all beings here.

[296]

डाल भइहैं मूल तें, मूल डाल के माहिं ।
सबहि पड़ें जब भरम में, मूल डाल कछु नाहिं ॥

The branch is born of the root
The root is in the branch
When all the world is in confusion
Branch nor root you catch!

Though the branch grows out of the root of the tree, and the root exists also in the branch, because everyone is groping in the dark neither the root nor the branch is taken notice of. Kabīr implies that due to ignorance man does not know the essence of things.

[297]

देखो कर्म कबीर का, कछू पूरब जनम का लेख ।
जाका महल न मुनि लहै, सो दोसत किया अलेख ॥

Says Kabīr,
Scan the deeds of the present life
And deeds of the past one
You will perceive what saints could not
Befriending the Unknown.

Kabīr indicates that one will be able to comprehend what befalls him in life and why if he scans the deeds of his present life and knows about the deeds of the past one by befriending the unknown. He implies that man cannot avoid the outcome of his deeds in the present and past life also. By 'unknown' Kabīr implies the Lord and indicates that by taking refuge in Him man will become aware of the deeds of his past life, and thereby shed all strife of the mind.

[298]

गुर सेबा जन बंदगी, हरि सुमिरन बेराग ।
यह चारों तबही मिलें, पूरन होबे भाग ॥

Service to the preceptor, meditation on the Lord
And also non-attachment

These and selfless help to others
     You can achieve if backed by fate.

It is very difficult to succeed in the four most rewarding tasks of rendering service to the preceptor, meditation on the Lord, non-attachment to worldly connections and selfless help to others unless one is backed by fate, indicates Kabīr. In other words, one will be considered lucky if he can succeed in all these directions.

[299]

हिंदु कहूं तो मैं नहीं, मुसलमान भी नाहिं ।
पांच तत का पूतला, गेबो खेले माहिं ॥

I am neither Muslim nor Hindu
     None of them I am
A doll made of the five elements
     To play some funny game!

Kabīr disowns that he is either Hindu or Muslim. He is neither, he declares. He asserts that he is just a doll made of the five elements (viz. earth, water, air, heat and void) meant to play some funny games. He implies that man plays a very insignificant role in God's vast universe. He also asserts that basically or from birth no man belongs to any particular faith or cult. He is born as man alone.

[300]

देस देसांतर मैं फिरौं, मानुस बड़ा सुकाल ।
जा देख सुख ऊपजै, ताका बड़ा दुकाल ॥

In many a land at home and abroad
     I found men are plentiful
But rarely the one whose very sight
     Made me cheerful.

The innate goodness of a man shows up in his face and eyes and the heart gladdens on seeing such a person. Such men are extremely rare, Kabīr affirms.

GLOSSARY

OF NON-ENGLISH WORDS AND OBSCURE EXPRESSIONS
USED IN THE COUPLETS

No. (1)   Guru: Spiritual preceptor of Hindu faith.

           Govind: One of the names of the Supreme God of Hindu Pantheon.

No. (22)   Mehadī: Indian name of a thorny plant whose green leaves are used after pasting for reddening the nails and palms of young maidens.

No. (30)   Three 'guṇas'   The three essential qualities of *sattva* (truth), *rajas* (worldly) and *tamas* (dark or impure) signifying the three categories of humans.

No. (41)   Kājal   A kind of dark preparation of local raw-materials for anointing the eyelids and also known as *kājara*.

No. (43)   Sever and   Symbolically, complete self-surrender to the Lord.
           offer head

No. (50)   Alchemy   'Rasāyana' used in the original couplet is an alchemic substance used for purifying baser metals etc. Kabīr implies that the Name of the Lord is the most effective alchemic substance to purify man by instant effect.

No. (56)   Cross the bar   Attain salvation after crossing the worldly ocean of life's journey.

No. (64)   Karṇa   A valiant warrior of *Mahābhārata* fame who fought on the side of Kauravas. He was well-known for his benevolence.

No. (69)   Diamond   Symbolically refers to the Lord, being most precious like diamond-

No. (71)	Five naughty sons	The five enemies of man living in him—anger, lust, greed, pride and attachment. (Also see Verse Nos. 149 & 241)
No. (72)	Svāti rain	Rainfall when the *svāti* star is in the sky. It is believed that pearls develop in the sea shells after they swallow some rain drops during that period. (Also see Verse No. 106)
No. (80)	Sense enemies	*Māyā, lobha, kāma, krodha* and *ahankāra* corresponding to attach-ment, greed, lust, anger and pride, respectively.
No. (89)	'Skin not fit for the drum'	While the hide of cow, goat etc., are used for drums to produce sound, human skin is not.
No. (93)	Viṣṇu	The highest God of Hindu Pan-theon.
No. (100)	Other One	Signifying the Supreme Soul or God (*Paramātmā*).
No. (117)	When waves abate	When mind's agitation subsides and it becomes steady and stable.
No. (118)	Māyā	Illusion, an important concept of Indian Philosophy. In common parlance the word is used to de-note excessive attachment to a person (woman) or property (riches).
No. (119)	Lamp Game	Refers to *Māyā* or bonds of earth. Birds or insects hunted for food.
No. (126)	Cātaka	A little Indian bird of lark varie-ty. It is said they drink only rain drops falling from the sky. An-other name for the bird is *papīhā*.
No. (134)	Paun	Synonym for 'life', the breath of life symbolically called 'bird'.

No. (149)	Enemies five	Lust, anger, greed, worldly attachment and pride. (See also Verse No. 71)
No. (151)	Kājara	See Verse No. 41.
No. (160)	maund	A measure equal to about fifty litres.
No. (162)	Cupadī	Baked *āṭṭā* (wheat powder) bread on which ghee (milkfat) is spread thinly.
No. (167)	Sūda	Abbreviation for 'Śūdra', the lowest of the four main castes of the Hindu hierarchy, Brahmin at the top. Kabīr designates those who devised the caste as deceptors. In his view all are human, none high, none low.
No. (169)	Yogāsana	A form of Yogic exercise done by a class of ascetics and also by others.
No. (169)	Bullock of the oilman	The animal engaged in driving the old type of wooden oil mill by going round and round. When taken home at the end of the day's work for feeding the animal, though all the time near home, presumes that he has travelled a long distance to reach home.
No. (177)	Satī	Widow who is made to sacrifice herself in the funeral pyre of her deceased husband. This ancient system was in vogue in Kabīr's days.
No. (180)	Brahmin	The highest caste in Hindu Society. (Also see Verse No. 167)
No. (183)	Hunter, leopard and thief	These three bow down too much with evil intention—the hunter for killing the prey, the leopard for leaping upon its prey, and the thief for concealing his presence while committing theft.

No. (185)	Cow	Symbolic for life force or soul of man.
No. (192)	Five little birds	The five sense enemies in man viz. lust, ire, greed, attachment and pride. (Also see Verse Nos. 71 & 149)
	wily hunter	Implies, symbolically, death.
No. (193)	far off home	It is believed that the soul in man (*Jīvātmā*) is a part and parcel of the Supreme Soul (*Paramātmā* or God) whose abode is believed to be heaven, which is said to be a far off region.
No. (202)	Biraha	Literally *biraha* means separation. In this case it refers to the deep yearning of the soul (*Jīvātmā*) for union with *Paramātmā* (Supreme Soul or God) of which it is a part.
No. (210)	Gaṅgodaka	Ganges river water considered sacred by the Hindus, and called by that name—*Gaṅgodaka*.
No. (216)	Phālguna	The month corresponding to February which heralds the spring season in India.
No. (218)	Palāsa	A tree yielding bright red and fragranceless flowers.
	Sandal	A tree yielding sweet smelling wood.
No. (224)	Bonded	Literally bound to earth, as opposed to one who has earned his salvation.
No. (240)	Khicadī	A rice preparation in which pulse, some vegetable slices, and spieces are added and cooked together.
No. (245)	You lose your head by keeping it	Implying that if one is not able to offer himself to the Lord in self-surrender he will not be able to attain salvation.

No. (246)	Rāma	Name of God incarnated as 'Rāma' according to Hindu mythology. Kabīr calls his presiding Deity or Supreme God by that name.
	Rahīm	Name of God of kindness in Islamic theology.
No. (247)	Root	The essence of things. Kabīr implies by root the Lord Supreme, and indicates that man should take refuge in Him.
	Eats ripe fruits to fill	Enjoys the blessing of the Lord.
No. (253)	Śiva & Śaṅkara	Synonyms for Maheśvara, the god of death and destruction in Hindu mythology.
No. (257)	Celā	Disciple of Hindu Guru or preceptor.
	Murīd	Disciple of Islamic preceptor or 'Pīr'.
	Pīr	Spiritual preceptor of Islamic faith.
No. (260)	Lamp is burning	So long as man is alive. The burning of the lamp has been used symbolically for existence of life. "When oil dries up and the lamp goes out" signifies man's death.
No. (265)	True hero	Devotee unflinching in his devotion to the Lord.
No. (270)	Kābbā	The principal place of Islamic pilgrimage in Arabia. Another name for Mecca.
No. (275)	One	Signifying the human soul.
No. (277)	Who dies before death	Refers to those who kill their pride and thus become deathless by earning salvation during life time.
	Kali Yuga	The last of the four *yugas* (Ages) according to Hindu mythology, noted for rise of sin—said to be current now.

No. (279)	If you burn your house	Symbolically banishing greed and attachment.
	Dead devouring demise	If man banishes or kills his greed and attachment he becomes death-less thus symbolically defeating or killing death itself. The dead greed and attachment defeat or kill death.
No. (281)	Drop of water	Symbolically, the soul of man.
	Sea	Symbolically, the Supreme Soul or God.
No. (288)	Cakora (Cakuā)	A little bird too much attached to the moon. Synonym for *cakora*.
No. (292)	Burnt my house	Forsake attachment to hearth and home.
No. (299)	five elements	Earth, water, heat, air and void which the human body is made of.

SELECT BIBLIOGRAPHY

Chaturvedi, Parasuram, *Uttar Bharat ki Sant Parampara* (in Hindi), 1960.

Das, Shyam Sunder, *Kabir Granthavali* (in Hindi), Nagri Pracharini Sabha, Kashi, 1960.

Dwivedy, Acharya Hazari Prasad, *Kabir* (in Hindi), Rajkamal Prakashan, New Delhi, 1980.

Gupta, Mataprasad, *Kabir Granthavali* (in Hindi), Sahitya Bhavan Ltd., Allahabad, 1985.

Hari, Biyogi, *Sant Sudha Saar* (in Hindi), Sant Sahitya Mandal Prakashan, 1969.

Mishra, Bhubaneswar, *Sant Sahitya Aur Sadhana* (in Hindi), National Publishing House, Delhi, 1964.

Singh, Puspapal, *Kabir Granthavali* (in Hindi), 1964.

Tagore, Rabindranath, *Poems of Kabir* (in English), Macmillan, India, 19th ed., 1985.

Trigunavat, Govind, *Kabir ki Vichaardhaaraa*, (in Hindi), Sahitya Niketan, Kanpur, 1981.

Verma, Ram Kumar, *Kabir—Biography and Philosophy* (in English), Prints India, New Delhi, 1977.

Verma, Ram Kumar, *Kabir ka Rahasyavad* (in Hindi), Sahitya Bhavan, Allahabad, 1984.